SHAMBHALA DRAGON EDITIONS

The dragon is an age-old symbol of the highest spiritual essence, embodying wisdom, strength, and the divine power of transformation. In this spirit, Shambhala Dragon Editions offers a treasury of readings in the sacred knowledge of Asia. In presenting the works of authors both ancient and modern, we seek to make these teachings accessible to lovers of wisdom everywhere.

MASTERING THE ART OF WAR

Zhuge Liang & Liu Ji

TRANSLATED AND EDITED BY
THOMAS CLEARY

SHAMBHALA
BOSTON & LONDON
1989

Shambhala Publications, Inc.
Horticultural Hall
300 Massachusetts Avenue
Boston, Massachusetts 02115

9 8 7 6 5

Printed in the United States of America on acid-free paper ⊗

Distributed in the United States by Random House, Inc.,
and in Canada by Random House of Canada Ltd

Library of Congress Cataloging-in-Publication Data
Mastering the art of war.
1. Sun-tzu, 6th cent. B.C. Sun tzu ping fa.
2. Military art and science. I. Chu-ko, Liang, 181–234.
II. Liu, Chi, 1311–1375. III. Cleary, Thomas F., 1949–
U101.S96M37   1989   355.02   89-10264
ISBN 0-87773-513-1

CONTENTS

CONTENTS

CONTENTS

NOTE ON PRONUNCIATION

The Chinese proper names in this book are transliterated in Pinyin, the most widely accepted method of romanization for Chinese. In actual usage, Chinese phonetics are so complex that a detailed treatment of Chinese pronunciation is outside the scope of this book. For the comfort and ease of the reader, however, it is useful to note a few letters that are commonly used in Pinyin spelling but are relatively uncommon in English and are given different values.

There are five consonants that are typically found to cause problems because of their special usage: c, q, x, z and zh. The following chart represent rough equivalents to these consonants in English:

c resembles ts

q resembles ch

x resembles sh

z resembles dz

zh resembles j

MASTERING
THE ART OF WAR

TRANSLATOR'S
INTRODUCTION

Skilled warriors of old were subtle
Mysteriously powerful
So deep they were unknowable
Tao Te Ching

Be extremely subtle
Even to the point of formlessness
Be extremely mysterious
Even to the point of soundlessness
Thereby you can be the director
Of an opponent's fate
The Art of War

Change and movement have their times; safety and danger
are in oneself. Calamity and fortune, gain and loss, all
start from oneself. Therefore those who master change are
those who address themselves to the time. For those who
address themselves to the time, even danger is safe; for
those who master change, even disturbance is orderly.
The Book of Balance and Harmony

The study and practice of strategic living in the midst of all
situations and events have been a central concern of practical
philosophers of all the great cultures since ancient times. In
China, one of the oldest living civilizations on earth, the
classical philosophers concerned themselves with humanity's

1

struggle to survive and find security in the midst of endless change and movement. Many of the ancient teachers of wisdom were also artisans and scientists, seeking new strategies for living in their study of human nature and destiny; others were political and even military leaders, studying the most complex and difficult problems of society.

According to the philosophers of ancient China, when the pristine sociability of humanity had become distorted by personal ambitions, it fell into a state of perpetual inner war. This war manifested itself in social unrest, class conflict, and eventually armed aggression. From this time on the philosophers made it their particular concern to study mechanisms of human conflict and develop their understanding into practical sciences of crisis management.

For this reason, very early classical Chinese literature is already examining war deliberately, not only from the point of view of when and how to prosecute war, but also from the point of view of its impact on society and the resulting ethical implications. The *Yin Convergence Classic*, for example, is considered a most ancient Taoist text, believed to antedate even the *Tao Te Ching* ("The Way and Its Power"), having such consequent prestige that it is avidly studied by both social strategists and mystics: in a typically laconic manner this short work already summarizes the attitudes to war later adopted by various schools of thought, including the perennial Taoist and Confucian philosophies: "Cut off one wellspring, that of profiteering," the classic says, "and that is ten times better than mobilizing the army."

Later the *Tao Te Ching*, undoubtedly the most famous pure Taoist classic, elaborated on the theme of greed as the motive force underlying aggression:

> When the world has the Way,
> Running horses are retired to till the fields.
> When the world lacks the Way,
> War-horses are bred in the countryside.
> No crime is greater than approving of greed,
> No calamity is greater than discontent,
> No fault is greater than possessiveness.

The same fundamental theme is carefully elaborated in the *I Ching* ("Book of Changes"), another early Chinese classic, one that is devoted, as the title suggests, to a science of mastering change, the basic fact of life. The same passage of the *Yin Convergence Classic* goes on to explain that cutting off the wellspring of greed begins at home: "Introspect three times day and night, and that is ten thousand times better than mobilizing the army." This is also one meaning of the now proverbial line of the *Tao Te Ching:* "The journey of a thousand miles begins with the first step," which from the original may also be translated, "The journey of a thousand miles begins at your feet."

Later classics also follow this theory that social reform must begin within the individual, and the implication that inward renewal of conscience is ultimately more effective than external imposition of law. For this reason Chinese philosophers concluded that education was of ever-increasing importance to society as a whole. They often had radically different ideas about the kind of education they considered necessary, but all of them agreed to include the study of conflict. And as it turned out, in spite of the variety of their ideas on other subjects, the ancient Chinese philosophers often came to the same conclusions on conflict. Thus the classics on strategy in conflict, such as the famous handbook known as *The Art of War* by Sun Tzu, generally contain an amalgam of the major philosophies of ancient China, particularly those derived from the *I Ching*.

The history of warfare in China reaches back into ancient myths representing great warriors as mystics and magicians whose legendary struggles came to typify the philosophers' ideals of justice and social service in the early emergence of civilization. The realities of war in historical times were never quite as clear and simple as the paradigms of legend, but certain fundamental images and concepts were tenaciously held by politicans, philosophers, and warriors throughout the centuries in their thinking about contention and conflict.

China is a heterogeneous civilization with vast territories encompassing and bordering on an even greater variety of peoples. Its history is marked by centuries of warfare both civil and foreign. The persistence of certain causes and patterns of conflict over nearly three thousand years makes the study of warfare and the philosophy of the warriors potentially instructive and even enlightening, bringing out the essence of conflict.

Reduced to simple formulae, the power struggles that underlie three thousand years of warfare in China represent elaborations of a few basic antagonisms. The early warfare of Chinese folklore was tribal war among the peoples who lived or moved along the Yellow River. Certain tribes came to dominate others, until relatively large and quite powerful confederations developed along the Yellow River during the third and second millennia B.C.E. During the extended lives of these confederations, warfare broke out among regional interests in the control of the clans who organized and dominated them. This gradually intensified in frequency and violence, culminating in a prolonged period of virtually continuous warfare appropriately known as the era of the Warring States, which lasted from the fifth through the third centuries B.C.E.

A relentless campaign of the late third century finally ended these interstate wars and created a united China for the first time in history. This was followed by wars of expansion, which are analogous to the ancient tribal wars through which the proto-Chinese people originally established dominance over the Yellow River basin. Under the united Chinese regime, warfare between the ruled and the rulers became a typical pattern of conflict, in which regionalism continued to play a part.

Struggles between local interests and central control, and between overclasses and underclasses, played themselves out in various combinations and elaborations of these elements through countless civil and foreign intrigues and wars in the centuries to come. Added to this were clan and family rivalries, as well as political conflicts among the intelligentsia, palace eunuchs, and imperial in-laws. On greater and smaller scales, the race for power and possessions became a distinct facet of human events, to which practical philosophers responded with a science of security and strategic action.

Some of the most poignant statements on war and warriorhood originate in the classic *Tao Te Ching*, generally thought to have been compiled during the early to middle Warring States era. In the characteristic fashion of Taoism, this popular text seeks out the confluence of ethical and practical wisdom:

> Weapons, being instruments of ill omen,
> Are not the tools of the cultured,
> Who use them only when unavoidable,
> And consider it best to be aloof.
> They win without beautifying it:
> Those who beautify it
> Enjoy killing people.
> Those who enjoy killing people
> Cannot get their will of the world.
>
> When you are in ascendancy of power,
> You handle it as you would a mourning:
> When you have killed many people,
> You weep for them in sorrow.
> When you win a war,
> You celebrate by mourning.

The same classic also describes the skilled warrior in similar terms, as the antithesis of bravado and violence:

> Skilled warriors of old were subtle,
> Mysteriously powerful,
> So deep they were unknowable.
> Just because they are unknowable,
> I will try to describe them:
> Their wariness was as that of one
> Crossing a river in winter;
> Their caution was as that of one
> In fear of all around.
> They were serious as guests,
> Relaxed as ice at the melting point.
> Simple as uncarved wood,
> Open as the valleys,
> They were inscrutable as murky water.

This Taoist stream of thought had a distinct influence on the strategic outlook of *The Art of War*, and elements of its penetrating criticism of tyranny in all forms also appear in the ideas of the later Warring States philosophers Mozi and Mencius. Both of these thinkers, especially Mozi, were activists, noted for their strong views on warfare.

Teaching that social well-being derives from universal love, Mozi described warfare as mass murder and ridiculed the states of his time for punishing individual thefts and murders while rewarding pillage and massacre. Mozi himself designed war machinery and organized a highly mobile brigade of ascetic religious warriors to go to the rescue of small states victimized by larger ones. After his passing, Mozi's followers continued this tradition until about the end of the Warring States era.

Mencius, who lived somewhat after the time of Mozi, is famous for his elaboration of the teachings of the great educator Confucius. Whereas Mozi had focused his attention on interstate conflicts, Mencius was more concerned with class conflicts. His work strongly upholds the principle and practice of identity of interests as essential to social and political health. Accordingly, Mencius repudiated the last vestiges of ancient beliefs in the divine right of kings, and articulated the moral basis of rebellion by oppressed peoples.

Both Mozi and Mencius came to be regarded by Taoists as of their number in some sense, as were Confucius and other early philosophers who wrote the *I Ching* and *The Art of War*. In the second century B.C.E., all of these schools of thought were incorporated in some way into one book, the distinguished Taoist classic known as *The Masters of Huainan*. The subject matter of this extraordinary book covers a wide range of inquiry including politics, sociology, ecology, biology, and psychology, weaving them into a unified science of life. *The Masters of Huainan* combines the teachings of the *I Ching*, the *Tao Te Ching*, and the higher teachings of *The Art of War*, as typified in a story on a way to practice the dictum of the last-mentioned classic of strategy, that "to win without fighting is best."

When the state of Jin marched on the state of Chu, the grandees of Chu asked the king to attack, but the king said, "Jin did not attack us during the reign of our former king; now that Jin is attacking us during my reign, it must be my fault. What can be done for this disgrace?"

The grandees said, "Jin did not attack us in the time of

6

previous ministries; now that Jin is attacking us during our administration, it must be our fault."

The king of Chu bowed his head and wept. Then he rose and bowed to his ministers.

When the people of Jin heard about this, they said, "The king of Chu and his ministers are competing to take the blame on themselves; and how easily the king humbles himself to his subordinates. They cannot be attacked."

So that night the Jin army turned around to go home.

This is why the *Tao Te Ching* says, "Who can accept the disgrace of a nation is called ruler of the land."

The Masters of Huainan relates another anecdote to illustrate a corollary principle of *The Art of War*, to the effect that when contention escalates to conflict there is already loss even in victory, and this can lead to even greater loss even after it has ended:

> The Martial Lord of Wei asked one of his ministers what had caused the destruction of a certain nation-state. The minister said, "Repeated victories in repeated wars."
>
> The Martial Lord said, "A nation is fortunate to win repeated victories in repeated wars. Why would that cause its destruction?"
>
> The minister said, "Where there are repeated wars, the people are weakened; when they score repeated victories, rulers become haughty. Let haughty rulers command weakened people, and rare is the nation that will not perish as a result."

Eventually the whole range of Chinese thought on the practicalities of life was inherited by the Chan Buddhists, who subjected the understanding of every school of ideas to the most rigorous examination in order to cull the essence and sense of each one. Thus one of the most excellent presentations of the hierarchy of Chinese philosophies of war can be found in the writings of the illustrious eleventh-century Buddhist Mingjiao, who was a scholar and historian as well as a master of Chan Buddhist mysticism:

> The use of arms is for dealing with criminal acts; it comes from humanitarianism and is based on justice. It comes

from humanitarianism in the sense of sympathy for those whose lives are being disrupted, and is based on justice in the sense of stopping violence.

When violence is stopped justly, there is mutual realignment, not mutual disturbance. When those whose lives are disrupted are pitied for humanitarian reasons, plans are made to foster life, not to kill.

Therefore the armed actions of the idealized leaders of ancient times are called corrective punishments and campaigns for justice.

When social cohesion waned and the Warring States era set in, the course of military science changed: humanitarianism and justice faded out; instead military affairs came from violence and went to treachery. Strong states became unrestrained through militarism, large states grew arrogant because of their armies, angry states used their weapons to incite disturbance, and greedy states used their armed forces to invade others.

"Military action is a perverse affair, used by the civilized only when unavoidable." Therefore sages value moral power, not military power. This is why those who understand military science should not run the world alone.

"Putting on armor is not the way to promote a country's welfare; it is for eliminating violence."

"A lost country wars with weapons; a dictatorship wars with cunning; a kingdom wars with humanitarian justice; an empire wars with virtue; a utopia wars with nondoing."

A later Chan Buddhist, also an enlightened scholar and poet, added other points of view to his predecessor's account of the classical philosophies of war. He recorded his observations in hauntingly beautiful poetry while hiding in the mountains after falling victim to an intrigue. A strong Taoist element, part of the ancient heritage of Chan Buddhism, is evident in the poet's incisive vision of history and impartial understanding of the beauty and tragedy of contending interests in the course of human life.

Impressions on Reading History

The enlightened and the good get things done only from
time to time

8

While petty bureaucrats always support one another.
Once slanderers and flatterers get their wishes
Sages and philosophers are deterred.
The Great Process makes myriad beings
Of countless different types.
Fragrant and foul are not put together
The humane and the violent apply different norms.
If you put them together
How can they get along?

Lament of a Soldier's Wife

You're better off grass by the roadside
Than wife to a soldier at war.
The wedding bed not even warm
Her man's now on the northern front.
She remembers the day they parted
How the snow flew o'er the landscape
Bow and arrows heavy at his side
Ice splitting his horse's hooves
He is so far from home
How can they hope to meet?
It saddens her even to see sun and moon
That shine on both her and her man
Pining and pining she longs
When will it ever end?
Every night in labored dreams
Her spirit crosses the northern front so far.
But there is a rule in the army
To be careful all of the time
They cannot think of home and family
But work mindlessly for defense
Since ancient times men loyal to duty
All have learned to die.

THE ART OF WAR AND THE
I CHING:
STRATEGY AND CHANGE

The Art of War and the *I Ching* are two perennial Chinese classics, ancient books that have been studied by civil and military strategists throughout the ages in China and neighboring Asian countries. *The Art of War* includes the cultural within the martial; the *I Ching* includes the martial within the cultural. In classical Chinese political ideology, military strategy was a subordinate branch of social strategy. Accordingly, the first line of national defense against disruption of order by external or internal forces was believed to lie in the moral strength of a united people. It was further maintained that people could be united by policies that fostered the general welfare. Since unity was distinguished from uniformity in the *I Ching*, purist ideology maintained that these policies had to be adapted to the time, place, and people they were supposed to serve.

The following studies of *The Art of War* survey both ideas and events in the philosophy and application of conflict management according to this tradition. The connection between the philosophy and organizational science of *The Art of War* and the even more ancient *I Ching* is cited in the introduction to my translation of *The Art of War*. In order to put this classic of strategy in its philosophical perspective, it is logical to begin with the teachings on contention and military action outlined in the *I Ching* itself.

To many readers both East and West, the *I Ching* may be familiar as an ancient book of omens, used for millennia as a fortune-telling handbook. It is still undoubtedly used for prognostication, but this practice has not been endorsed by leading philosophers or political scientists. Divination has been explicitly prohibited by military scientists at least as far back in history as *The Art of War* itself.

For the social scientist, the *I Ching* is a book of strategic assessments, whose design is supposed to help the individual lead a more rational and effective life. Its structure is based on a quadrangle of four fundamental sets of ideas, on which revolves a cycle of three hundred and sixty states of opportunity. The number three hundred and sixty corresponds to the days of the lunar year, which in turn is emblematic of totality and completeness. These states are grouped into sixty major configurations, represented by symbolic signs, or hexagrams, consisting of six elements each.

Every hexagram is given a name and a theme, which stands for some aspect of life and development in the midst of change. This is accompanied by observations and images of possibility and change that can take place within human relationships under such conditions, when analogous opportunities develop in the course of events. The six elements within each hexagram are also accompanied by observations and images that further analyze the theme from different points of view, according to the various relative positions in which people may find themselves under given conditions.

The two themes in the *I Ching* that are most prominently relevant to a study of *I Ching* influence in *The Art of War* would be those of the sixth and seventh hexagrams, "Contention" and "The Army." Considered in succession according to the traditional order of study used for temporal events, the observations of these two *I Ching* themes form an outline of classical thinking on the structure of conflict response.

The statement of the *I Ching* on the hexagram for "Contention" reads, "In contention there is sincerity." Cheng Yi, one of the best *I Ching* readers in history, an idealist interpreter under the influence of Taoism and Chan Buddhism, explains this idea simply by saying that "Contention arises because of need." With customary ambiguity, this remark applies to both predatory and defensive warfare.

In its overall symbolism, the hexagram for "Contention" shows internal desire and outward strength. This combination is taken to represent the greedy and aggressive possibilities in human psychology and behavior that lead to contention. Thus the "need" Cheng Yi calls the source from which contention arises may be understood to refer to the internal forces compelling an aggressor as well as the external forces necessitating defense against aggression.

In the code of ethics outlined in the *I Ching*, contention is considered justifiable when it is in resistance to oppression, or in opposition to suffering caused by greed and aggression. This principle is confirmed in all three of the major Ways of Chinese thought, in Confucianism and Taoism as well as in Buddhism. Therefore "contention that is just" also arises because of need. This is the "sincerity in contention" of which the *I Ching* speaks. Cheng Yi says, "Without sincerity and truthfulness, contention is merely intrigue and leads to misfortune."

This code is also reflected in the practical teachings of *The Art of War*. In the chapter on "Maneuvering Armies," Master Sun says, "To be violent at first and wind up fearing one's people is the epitome of ineptitude." In the chapter on "Fire Attack," he says, "A government should not mobilize an army out of anger, leaders should not provoke war out of wrath. Act when it is beneficial, desist if it is not."

The *I Ching*'s statement on "Contention" continues, "[When] obstructed, be careful to be balanced, for that will lead to good results. Finality leads to bad results." Cheng Yi says:

> People who contend match their reasoning with others in anticipation of a decision. Though they may be sincere and truthful, [if there is contention, that means] they are necessarily obstructed; something must be unresolved, for if that were not the case, the matter would already be clear and there would be no dispute.
>
> Since the matter is not yet settled, one cannot necessarily say whether it will turn out well or badly. Therefore there is great concern that an auspicious balance be achieved and maintained. If you achieve balance, that bodes well. "Finality leads to bad results" means that if you conclude affairs with unmitigated finality, that bodes ill.

On the same principle, in the chapter on "Fire Attack" *The Art of War* says, "Anger can revert to joy, wrath can revert to delight, but a nation destroyed cannot be restored to existence, and the dead cannot be restored to life. Therefore an enlightened government is careful about this, a good military leadership is alert to this."

In its technical sense in *I Ching* philosophy, a state of balance or centeredness means an attitude that is not affected by emotion. According to the traditional formula as cited in *The Book of Balance and Harmony*, a neo-Taoist classic based on the *I Ching*, "Before emotions arise is called balance; when emotions arise yet are moderate, this is called harmony." Traditional Taoist teaching understands *balance* to mean being objective and impartial. In the classical formula of "balance and harmony," this objective impartiality is always placed first, because it is held to be the practical means whereby harmony can subsequently be attained.

Because of the serious consequences of decisions made in contention, the *I Ching* adds to its statement, "It is beneficial to see a great person." This is a stock phrase, traditionally understood to mean that real wisdom and knowledge are essential and cannot be replaced by emotional opinion. Cheng Yi describes great people, or people of wisdom, as those who "can settle disputes with firm understanding that is balanced and true."

The Art of War also places great emphasis on the importance of mature guidance, which becomes increasingly critical in times of conflict and crisis: "Leadership is a matter of intelligence, trustworthiness, humaneness, courage, and sternness" ("Strategic Assessments"). According to classical philosophers, impartial wisdom is valuable to all parties in a dispute, insofar as loss already starts with contention and is maximized when contention becomes conflict. Furthermore, for those already involved in struggle, effective deployment of energies depends on guidance or leadership to concentrate them.

In both classical and modern terms, the *I Ching*'s statement that "it is beneficial to see great people" is also taken to refer to the importance of education, exposing the population to the thoughts of great minds; this too is a form of leadership, one which philosophers believed should also inform the exercise of live personal leadership.

The final word of the *I Ching*'s observation on the general theme of "Contention" says, "It is not beneficial to cross great rivers." According to Cheng Yi, this means that one should take safety precautions and not become reckless in contention. According to the tradition of strategists, knowledge of conditions is the basis of caution and preparedness: in its chapter on "Planning a Siege," *The Art of War* says, "If you do not know others and do not know yourself, you will be imperiled in every single battle." In actual conflict, this naturally extends to matters of logistics: in the chapter on "Doing Battle," *The Art of War* also says, "When a country is impoverished by military operations, it is because of transporting supplies to a distant place. Transport supplies to a distant place, and the populace will be impoverished."

The remark that "it is not beneficial to cross great rivers" in contention can also be read as a restatement of the basic principle of ethical contention that distinguishes it from invasive and aggressive action. In the chapter on "Terrain," *The Art of War* says, "One advances without seeking glory, retreats without avoiding blame, only protecting people." Similarly, the Taoist classic *The Masters of Huainan* says of adventurism, "Covetous people with many desires are lulled to sleep by power and profit, seduced into longing for fame and status. They wish to rise in the world through exceptional cunning, so their vitality and spirit are daily depleted and become further and further away."

The theme of "Contention" is further analyzed in the *I Ching*'s statements on each individual element of the hexagram. The first element shows lowliness and weakness. The statement of the text says, "When you do not persist forever in an affair, there is a little criticism, but the end is auspicious." Cheng Yi explains, "This is because contention in general is not something that should be prolonged; and weak people in low positions in particular hardly ever have any luck in contention."

The Art of War also reflects this principle of minimalism in its strategy; in the chapter on "Doing Battle," it says, "When you do battle, even if you are winning, if you continue for a long time it will dull your forces and blunt your edge; if you besiege a citadel, your strength will be exhausted. If you keep your armies out in the field for a long time, your supplies will be insufficient."

Cheng Yi's observation that powerless people in positions of weakness rarely have luck in contention also illustrates one reason why peasant uprisings throughout Chinese history have generally had among their leaders people from the intellectual, religious, military, or aristocratic classes. Cheng Yi says, "It is because there is corresponding assistance from a higher level that people in this position are able to refrain from persisting in an affair," since collaboration reduces conflict.

According to interpretation based on ethical idealism, the second element of the hexagram represents ambitious strength contending against a just order. Because this is contention motivated by personal desire and not by moral necessity, it is countermanded in the *I Ching*'s statement: "Not pressing your contention, go back to escape in your hometown; then you will be free from fault." Cheng Yi explains, "If you know that what is right and just is not to be opposed, and you go back home to live modestly, minding your own business, then you will be free from fault."

The third element of the "Contention" hexagram represents people who are pliable and weak in positions of relative strength. In the construction of a hexagram, the third position is strong insofar as it represents the highest place among the lower echelons. This corresponds to positions of subordinate authority, on more local and diffuse dimensions than the authority and power represented by the upper strata of the hexagram, which represent the higher and more concentrated levels of influence and leadership.

In "Contention," weakness at the top of the lower echelons is represented as characteristic of situations in which contention arises. The *I Ching*'s statement reads, "Living on past virtues, be steadfast." What the text means by "past virtues" may be the labor of one, two, three or more generations, generations of work forming the basis for the status of the present generation. From this point of view, to be steadfast (a stock *I Ching* term also meaning "chaste" and "true") can mean being careful not to lose what progress has been made, even over generations. In the context of the theme of this sign, to be steadfast or chaste would imply that losing or despoiling "past virtues" by contending for what is as yet unearned is something to be positively avoided.

In his interpretation, the idealist Cheng Yi gives a very specific understanding of what this line means to him in the context of one generation: "Living on past virtues," he says, "means living on what one has earned according to one's means." "Being steadfast," he continues, "means being firmly in control of oneself." Again, this line of the *I Ching* contains parallel social and strategic teachings. When *The Art of War* says, in its chapter on "Formation," that "good warriors take their stand on ground where they cannot lose," this also means that warriors are living on past accomplishments when they stand on secure ground in war.

Conversely, when *The Art of War* is reinterpreted sociologically, the meaning of this passage is identical to the understanding of the social idealist Cheng Yi—when warriors for good want to take their stand on ground where they cannot lose, they can do so only by living on what they have earned according to their means and by being in control of themselves.

This sort of parallelism of principle in different realms is characteristic of literature derived from or influenced by Taoist and Buddhist schools; and it is no doubt a factor in the perennial popularity of works such as the *I Ching* and *The Art of War* beyond their original contexts.

The *I Ching*'s reading for the third element of "Contention" also says, "Danger ends up all right." Cheng Yi explains, "Though you be in danger, if you know how to be wary, you will have good luck in the end." The word for *danger*, another standard *I Ching* term, also means "strict," "intense," and "diligent," encompassing reference to both problem and solution in one symbol, in accord with the *I Ching* principle of "using unfortunate events for good purposes," such as using stressful situations to arouse the willpower to overcome obstacles. *The Art of War*, in "Nine Grounds," says, "If they are to die there, what can they not do? Warriors exert their full strength. When warriors are in great danger, then they have no fear."

The final saying of the *I Ching* statement on the third element of "Contention" is, "If you work for the king, you will not accomplish anything." Cheng Yi interprets this to mean that people like those represented by this component should not arrogate to themselves the accomplishments that take place through participation in an existing system or a public forum. In this sense they need to recognize that they are "living on the past virtues" of many other people, and therefore not contend for special prominence or distinction simply on account of having done their work.

Echoing this principle of unobtrusive action and unassuming service, in the chapter on "Formation" *The Art of War* says, "In ancient times those known as good warriors prevailed when it was easy to prevail. Therefore the victories of good warriors are not noted for cleverness or bravery." This is also characteristic of Taoist philosophy; while undramatic, the indicated approach is held forth as a way to success: the *Tao Te Ching* says, "Plan for difficulty when it is still easy, do the great when it is still small."

The Art of War continues its description of the unassuming warriors of old by saying, "Therefore their victories in battle are not flukes. Their victories are not flukes because they position themselves where they will surely win, prevailing over those who have already lost." They take advantage of the structure and momentum in situations, so they do not seem to be doing anything themselves; this is one aspect of the Taoist "nondoing that does everything."

The fourth element of the "Contention" hexagram represents people with personal power at the bottom of the upper echelons. These are people within the established power structure who are forceful and contentious, people whose strength is not in balance. The *I Ching* addresses such situations in these terms: "Not pressing your contention, you return to order and change. Remain steadfast for good fortune." In a strategic reconstruction of this principle, the chapter on "Doing Battle" in *The Art of War* says, "It is never beneficial to a nation to have a military operation continue for a long time. Therefore those who are not thoroughly aware of the disadvantages in the use of arms cannot be thoroughly aware in the advantages in the use of arms."

Again using an idealistic ethical framework of interpretation, Cheng Yi explains that the contentious person within a duly established power structure has no one to contend with justly, therefore not pressing contention is a social duty. Returning to order, according to Cheng, means overcoming the emotions that feed contentiousness, so as to change the mentality to an evenminded, objective view of true facts. When this more positive attitude is stablized, there is normally better luck in social relations and consequent conflict resolution and avoidance.

Cheng Yi goes on to say, "Order means real truth; if you lose real truth, that is to go against order. So coming back to order is returning to truth. Ancient classics speak of the more obvious manifestations and consequences of going against order in terms of the brutalization and destruction of peoples." *The Art of War* says, "A nation destroyed cannot be restored to existence, the dead cannot be restored to life," merging utilitarian strategy and humanitarian ethics to conclude that in cases of contention "to win without fighting is best."

Cheng Yi continues: "The point is that when strength is not balanced correctly it behaves impulsively; it does not stay peacefully in place. Because it is not balanced correctly it is not steady; and it is precisely this insecurity that makes it contentious. If you do not press any contention that you should not press, and go back to find out the real truth, you will change insecurity into security, which is fortunate."

The fifth element of the "Contention" hexagram represents a strong and balanced leadership able to settle contention. The statement reads, "The contention is very auspicious." Cheng Yi interprets thusly: "Settling contention in a way that is balanced accurately is the way to results that are very auspicious and completely good." He also warns that the object of contention is not victory by any means, or at any cost: "Remember," he writes, "that there are cases where people are very lucky but the results are not entirely good."

Projecting the concept of "auspicious contention" into the

domain of crisis management, in the chapter on "Planning a Siege" *The Art of War* says, "Those who win every battle are not really skillful—those who render others' armies helpless without fighting are the best of all." In terms that can be seen as ethical, yet even when purely utilitarian still translate into humanitarian practicalities on the battlefield, *The Art of War* also says, "Act when it is beneficial, desist if it is not," and "do not fight when there is no danger" ("Fire Attack").

The sixth and topmost element of the "Contention" hexagram represents aggressive people in high positions, "at the peak of power and also at the end of contention," Cheng Yi says, "characteristic of those who bring contention to its ultimate conclusion." Here this means people who adamantly pursue contention to its final limit; Cheng Yi says, "When they indulge in their strength, and when they get desperate, people resort to contention, thus causing themselves trouble and even destroying themselves, a logical conclusion."

Liu Ji, the scholar-warrior whose recitals of history and military science are presented in the present volume, applies this principle to the monumental Sui dynasty. The Sui dynasty briefly united China in the late sixth century, after hundreds of years of civil and colonial warfare. Speaking of the second emperor, who inherited the empire his father had labored to consolidate, Liu Ji said, "It is not that his country was not large, nor that his people were not many. But he made a hobby of martial arts, and he liked to fight; so he practiced with his weapons every day, and went on endless expeditions to attack neighboring peoples. Then things took a turn, and his army was beaten while his cabinet opposed him. Is he not ridiculous to people of later generations? Had human rulers not better be careful?"

Aggressive and contentious people in high positions, used to getting their way, do not suffer only when they happen to fail; even in success they are in danger, for this success itself becomes an object of contention that continues to animate the aggressive tendencies of all people on this level. The *I Ching*'s statement on this point says, "Honor given you will be taken away from you three times before the day is out."

According to Cheng Yi, in a military, governmental, or

other institutional context, "even if people contend successfully to the end, until they are rewarded for service to the regime, this reward is still an object of contention—how can it be kept secure?" Liu Ji gives an excellent version of the traditional formulation of the answer among the rules of war related in his history stories: "When you have won, be as if you had not."

When contention is taken to its limit, it becomes conflict, and conflict taken to extremes leads to armament and war. Therefore the hexagram following "Contention" in the conventional order of the *I Ching* is the hexagram for "The Army." The word used for this sign has a whole family of meanings, including "a military force," "a military expedition," and "a military leader." From the last sense is derived another common usage of the same Chinese character, the meaning of "teacher, director, or master of an art or science."

The idea of the teacher fits in with the needs of military command or general crisis management; and the image of war is also used in both Taoism and Buddhism as a general metaphor for contending with any sort of difficulty, hardship, or problem, whether or not it involves interpersonal conflict. This concept also passed into the vocabulary of folklore and proverb.

The statement on the hexagram of "The Army" says, "For the army to be right, mature people are good. Then there is no fault." The implication is that there is a right way to use arms, and this leads back to the basic principle of ethical warfare according to the Taoist, Confucian, and Buddhist ways of thought: that war should be undertaken only as a last resort, and only in a just cause. This generally means defensive war, but it can also mean punitive war to stop the strong from bullying the weak. In either case, leadership has both a moral and a technical basis. The essays of Zhuge Liang translated in the present volume are particularly concerned with the characteristics and capacities of "mature people" capable of maintaining justice and order in military matters.

According to the classical traditions of China, war should be minimized even when it is justified. In ethical terms, this principle could be extended to mean war that is not minimized is for that very reason not just; in the strategic science of *The*

Art of War, prolonging or expanding hostilities unnecessarily is regarded as one of the major causes of self-destruction, which is considered neither ethical nor practical. This means in principle that the right way to carry out war, in the event of its necessity, is normally the right way from both humanitarian and utilitarian points of view.

History demonstrates clearly enough that in the absence of education from model moral leadership, war can easily turn into rapine and bloodlust, an outlet of frustration and oppression. On the other hand, without education from model technical leadership, armed forces can become clumsy and ineffective even if they are large in numbers. Therefore the *I Ching* says, "mature people are good," and adds, "then there is no fault." This parallel moral and technical leadership is constantly emphasized by Zhuge Liang and other noted strategists.

Cheng Yi explains this statement on "The Army" in these terms: "The course pursued by the army should be correct: if you raise an army and mobilize troops in a cause that is not right and only creates trouble, the people do not really obey, they are merely coerced. Therefore the guiding principle of the army should be uprightness."

Furthermore, not only does solidarity require that the cause be just in the eyes of those expected to fight for it, but competent leadership is also essential to direct and focus the process of struggle. Cheng Yi says, "Even if the army acts in the right way, the leaders must be mature to obtain good results. After all, there are those who are lucky but also faulty, and there are those who are faultless but still not lucky. To be lucky and also faultless is as mature as people can get. Mature people are stern and worthy of respect. If those who are to lead a group are not respected, trusted, and obeyed by the group, how can they get the people to follow willingly?"

Master Sun the Martialist makes the same point in the opening chapter of *The Art of War:* "The Way means inducing the people to have the same aim as the leadership, so that they will share death and share life, without fear of danger" ("Strategic Assessments"). Zhuge Liang's essays on generalship in the present volume stress the theme of harmonization among the different echelons of an organization as well as society in general. Liu Ji's war stories, in turn, include several cases of deliberate use of sternness and kindness in specific proportion to unify the minds of a military force.

The first element of the hexagram for "The Army" represents the beginning of mobilization. The statement of the original text says, "The army is to go forth in an orderly manner. Otherwise, doing well turns out badly." This theme of order permeates *The Art of War*, which views the functions and malfunctions of order from various angles. The great statesman and warrior Zhuge Liang is particularly famous for his insistence upon order in times of crisis. As a commander, he is said to have been strict yet impartial, with the result that his people regarded him with simultaneous awe and admiration, so that he was both honored and obeyed.

Two traditional Chinese concepts of the role or mode of human leadership in maintaining order were explained by a distinguished Chan Buddhist in these terms: "There are those who move people by enlightened virtue and those who make people obedient by the power of authority. It is like the phoenix in flight, which all the animals admire, or tigers and wolves stalking, which all the animals fear." In the martial tradition, authority means not only rank, but also personal power, awesome, charismatic, or both. Classical Chinese thought refers to this as a combination of the cultural and the martial, and this is considered standard for civilization after the prehistoric fall of humanity from pristine simplicity.

Even in the pacifist schools of Buddhism and Taoism, the martial image is retained for various practices, including critical analysis, intuitive penetration, and psychological purification, as well as hygienic and therapeutic exercises. It is well known, furthermore, that certain exercise movements are also used to train strength for combat, and other movements can be speeded up to produce martial effects.

One famous example of this is that of the Shaolin Boxers, a school recognized by Taoists but associated by them with Chan Buddhism. The appearance of fighting monks in China was in the defense of the country against invaders; followers of offshoots of these practices also kept theories of classical chivalry in their own codes, thus scattering the original principles of the *I Ching* throughout Chinese chivalric lore in the middle ages.

Cheng Yi also takes a characteristically moral view of the *I Ching*'s statement, "The army is to go forth in an orderly manner; otherwise doing well turns out badly." To the idealist Cheng, this reaffirms the importance of ethical human values in conflict. He says, "An 'orderly manner' means a combination of justice and reason. This means that the mission of the army is to stop disorder and get rid of violence. If the army acts unjustly, then even if it does well the affair turns out badly. In this sense, 'doing well' means winning victories; 'turning out badly' means killing people unjustly."

The second element of "The Army" hexagram represents the military leadership. It is placed in a subordinate position with respect to the civil leadership, representing the principle that the military exists to serve the nation and people, not the other way around. Cheng Yi says, "That means the leader of the army should be the leader only in the army." Zhuge Liang, who was both a civil and military director, also said, "Culture takes precedence over the martial."

The *I Ching*'s statement on the second element reads, "In the army, balanced, one is fortunate and blameless," meaning, "the leadership of a militia is lucky and blameless if it is balanced." Cheng Yi says, "Those who assume sole charge (of a militia) yet who manage to steer a balanced middle course are fortunate because of this, and are blameless."

In respect to the nature of military authority in the total context of society as symbolized by this hexagram, Cheng Yi defines one meaning of *balance* in these terms: "The point seems to be that if one presumes upon authority one strays from the right path of subordination; yet if one does not exercise authority there is no way to accomplish anything. Therefore it is best to find a balanced middle way." In abstract terms, a general stands for someone who has been entrusted with the responsibility for a task and, while exercising leadership and organizational skills to carry it through, does so with the awareness that field command, while completely in the hands of the general, is based on delegated authority. Although the qualities of leadership are essential in the leader of a delegation, it is the purpose and not the person that is of paramount importance in the whole event.

The statement of the *I Ching* on this element also says, "The king thrice bestows a mandate." This restates the constitutional imperative of *I Ching* culture, that the authorization for militia and military action comes from civil government. It is also taken to mean that if a militia or other special task force does its job well, then it is deemed trustworthy and therefore gives peace of mind to the populace. The practice of employing standing armies for public works projects originally grew out of this principle.

When this practice was employed in China, it brought armies closer to the general populace, often providing unique opportunities for contact between people from radically different areas of China, all the while giving the military—and by extension the government—a chance to establish public rapport by model behavior. Zhuge Liang was one of those known for his genius at winning popular support and was highly acclaimed as a civil administrator. His method of success seems to have been based to a large extent on his consistent practical application of Taoist and Confucian ethical principles.

This is something that distinguishes Zhuge Liang from many other intellectuals and administrators in Chinese history. Most such people did at least read or hear about these principles, but many used them only when it suited their immediate personal ambitions to do so. The epic *Tales of the Three Kingdoms,* a neoclassical historical novel strongly flavored with Taoist psychology, immortalizes the spiritual brilliance of Zhuge Liang as it satirizes and ridicules the warmongers who had a classical principle handy to rationalize every act of greed, treachery, and violence.

Cheng Yi explains the *I Ching*'s statement on bestowing mandates in these terms: "If it is employed in the best possible way, the army can accomplish works and make the world peaceful. It is for this reason that rulers entrust generals with important mandates time and again." In *The Art of War,* Master Sun also says, "Thus one advances without seeking glory, retreats without avoiding blame, only protecting people, to the benefit of the government as well, thus rendering valuable service to the nation" ("Terrain"). Zhuge Liang says, "A good general does not rely or presume on strength or power. He is not pleased by favor and does not fear vilification. He does not crave whatever material goods he sees, and he does not rape whatever women he can. His only intention is to pursue the best interests of the country." ("Loyalty in Generals").

In civilian terms, any delegated authority puts people in a similar position to that of the army in *I Ching* sociology; from the point of view of *I Ching* ethics, it is natural reason to carry out the duties of this delegated authority in an orderly and therefore efficient manner, without arrogating arbitrary authority to oneself. Cheng Yi says, "Even though it is in charge of itself, whatever the power of the army can bring about is all due to what is given to it by the leadership, and any accomplishment is all in the line of duty." The *I Ching* and derivative works on planning all stress the danger of the military leaving its subservient position and usurping the position of the civil authority. Any specialization can threaten society in the same way when it becomes self-serving instead of subservient to the whole body of society.

The Biblical saying that "the sabbath was made for man, and not man for the sabbath" is similar in this sense: reason says that institutions are created to provide service for humanity, not to advance the personal interests of those mandated to serve. In the same vein, Zhuge Liang writes, "When offices are chosen for persons, there is disorder; when persons are chosen for offices, there is order."

The proliferation of titles, offices, and emoluments to satisfy members of powerful and well-connected clans and interest groups was always one of the banes of Chinese government and religion, increasing the burdens on the taxpayers while hastening sclerosis in practical administration. Taoist philosophers said that this can happen in any domain of organized activity, of which national government is a highly visible and consequential example. Zhuge Liang emphatically stressed the idea that government should be streamlined, in accord with Taoist political theory, much of which is particularly designed for use in times of conflict and duress.

The third element of the hexagram for "The Army" symbolizes the secondary leaders within the army. The reading emphasizes the special importance of mutual understanding and order in the relationships on this level, as well as in relationships between this level of the chain of command and the central military leadership. This is also on the analogy of the subordination of the whole martial entity to the whole cultural entity.

The *I Ching*'s statement on the third element says, "It bodes ill for the army to have many bosses." Discord and competition in the lower ranks of command naturally weaken the whole body, especially by damaging and distorting the connection between the leadership and the common soldiery. Cheng Yi interprets, "The responsibility for a military expedition should be unified; one in a position of authority should concentrate on this." This also applies, like other *I Ching* metaphors, to other domains; in this case to the negative effects of extreme division and disunity on analogous levels of organization, from the organization of an individual life to the organization of a collective enterprise.

The Art of War also makes a point of the vulnerability inherent in disunity and directs its strategy at this weakness: in the chapter "Nine Grounds," Master Sun the Martialist says, "Those who are called the good militarists of old could make opponents lose contact between front and back lines, lose reliability between large and small groups, lose mutual concern for the welfare of the different social classes among them, lose mutual accommodation between the rulers and the ruled, lose enlistments among the soldiers, lose coherence within the armies." This is the familiar rule of "divide and conquer," amplifying the *I Ching* rule and carrying it into each dimension of an organization.

The fourth element of the hexagram for "The Army" represents being in a weak position and at a disadvantage in times of conflict. The statement says, "The army camps; no blame," meaning that it is normal to hold back or withdraw from an impossible position. Identical strategic principles are emphasized several times in *The Art of War*, as in the chapter on "Armed Struggle," which says, "Avoiding confrontation with orderly ranks and not attacking great formations is mastering adaptation." In the chapter on "Nine Grounds," it also says that good militarists of yore "went into action when it was advantageous, stopped when it was not."

The fifth element represents the civil leadership, whose authority is the source of the military's mandate. Since this serves as a general representation of delegation of authority for special purposes, the civil leadership is behind the scenes in "The Army." The *I Ching*'s statement, which simply summarizes the logic and ethic of warfare, begins. "When there are vermin in the fields, it is advantageous to denounce them; then there will be no fault." Cheng Yi understands this to mean eradicating active menaces to society, distinguishing this from acts of tyrannical aggression and paranoia: "The army should be mustered only when aggressors are hurting the people. . . . If it is a case like when vermin get into the fields and damage the crops, and it is justly appropriate to hunt them down, then hunt them down; act in this way and there will be no fault. Act at whim, thus harming the world, and the fault is great indeed. To 'denounce' means to make clear what has been done wrong, in order to stop it. Some martial tyrants have scoured the very mountains and forests for those whom they considered 'vermin,' but it was not that there were vermin in their own fields."

The *I Ching*'s statement concludes, "A mature person leads the army; there will be bad luck if there are many immature bosses, even if they are dedicated." This is a recapitulation of the general doctrine of the *I Ching* on the importance of wisdom in leadership and unity in organization. Cheng Yi says, "The way to mandate a general to direct an army calls for having a mature person lead the force. . . . If a group of immature people boss the army, then even if what they do is right, it will turn out badly."

The need for certain qualities in military leadership and unity in organization is among the first premises of *The Art of War*, and is a central theme of Zhuge Liang's writings on generalship. In his essay "Capacities of Commanders," Zhuge describes the greatest of military leaders in grandiose terms thoroughly consistent with *I Ching* idealism: "One whose humanitarian care extends to all under his command, whose trustworthiness and justice win the allegiance of neighboring nations, who understands the signs of the sky above, the patterns of the earth below, and the affairs of humanity in between, and who regards all people as his family, is a world-class leader, one who cannot be opposed."

The sixth and final element of the hexagram for "The Army" represents the end of the mission of the armed forces and the reintegration of warriors into civilian society. This can stand symbolically for the absorption of the results of any specialization into the whole body of society. In the context of civil or international warfare, here the *I Ching* reaffirms both the parallel and the contrast between martial and civil matters, as defined throughout its treatment of this theme.

Here, at the end of "The Army," the *I Ching* says, "The great leader has a command to start nations and receive social standing." Originally cast in a feudal setting, this statement illustrates a principle more generally understood here and now in bureaucratic or corporate contexts, for bureaucracies and conglomerates are the heirs of feudalism, though they rendered and consumed their parents some time ago.

Because many of the qualities needed for crisis management were also qualities needed for ordinary management, and because a complete education in China was believed to encompass both cultural and martial arts, a person might be both a military and a civilian leader, simultaneously or at different times. Zhuge Liang and Liu Ji are outstanding examples of individuals who were called upon to fulfill both military and civilian duties.

The *I Ching* implies that warriors rejoin civilization when war is over, thus avoiding the pitfalls of a socially isolated warrior caste and also contributing the knowledge, character, and experience gained in war to the society for which the war was waged. According to the *I Ching*'s statement, the ideal government contributes to this reintegration by entitling warriors according to their achievements. Cheng Yi says, "The great leader rewards the successful with entitlement, making them overseers of groups, and gives them social distinction for their capability." This is an example of the more general principle of meritocracy, a cornerstone of *I Ching* ideology written into the fundamentals of Confucian philosophy.

The underlying implication in the case of "The Army" and its end is the corollary doctrine, embraced by strategists like Zhuge Liang, that military personnel, and especially military leaders, should have a good general education as well as special technical and military training. In Chinese this is called the combination of *wen* and *wu*. *Wen*, or culture, deals with the cultivation of constructive social skills and values. *Wu*, or the martial, deals with both practical and theoretical sciences of crisis management. According to Chinese military science in the *I Ching*–Taoist tradition as represented by *The Art of War* and certain later adepts, balance in *wen* and *wu* is believed to be better for warriors even on campaigns and in combat, as well as when they are eventually reinstated into civilian society.

Therefore the *I Ching*'s statement concludes with the warning, "Petty people are not to be employed." In this context, the statement means that when it comes to integrating warriors into society, achievement in war should not be viewed in isolation as the only criterion of advancement, in disregard of the moral integrity and total person of the individual concerned. Cheng Yi says, "As for petty people, even if they have achieved, they are not to be employed. There is more than one way to raise an army, go on an expedition, and achieve success; those who do so are not necessarily good people."

Zhuge Liang is a model example of a leader in both realms, a beloved civil administrator as well as a distinguished strategist and general. His writings show a particularly deep savor of serious *I Ching* learning, combining Confucian and Taoist thought into an ethical yet pragmatic program for acute crisis management. Because of his fidelity to the classic traditions of humanitarian warrior-statesmen, the original roots and broad outlines of Zhuge Liang's thought can be traced in the fecund abstractions of the *I Ching* itself. This is also true of the work of Liu Ji, who goes even further than Zhuge Liang into the derivative traditions, especially the practical strategy and warrior ethos of *The Art of War*.

NOTES ON SOURCES

TAOIST WORKS CITED

The Yin Convergence Classic (Yinfujing). Included in *Vitality, Energy, Spirit: A Taoist Sourcebook*, by Thomas Cleary, forthcoming from Shambhala Publications.

Tao Te Ching

The Masters of Huainan (Huainanzi). A condensed translation of this text appears in *The Tao of Politics: Lessons of the Masters of Huainan*, by Thomas Cleary, forthcoming from Shambhala Publications.

The Book of Balance and Harmony (Zhonghoji). Translated by Thomas Cleary from North Point Press.

I CHING STUDIES

Material from and about the *I Ching* is excerpted from two translations by Thomas Cleary: *I Ching: The Tao of Organization* and *I Ching Mandalas* (both from Shambhala Publications).

HISTORICAL MATERIAL

For background on Liu Ji I used the Ming dynastic history and other standard reference works. For background on the Buddhist rebellions in which the Ming dynasty had its early roots, I am indebted to the extensive historical introduction of J. C. Cleary's *Zibo: China's Last Great Zen Master*. For corroboration of Liu Ji's recitals and other historical documentation, I am also indebted to Li Zhi's *Hidden Documents (Zang shu)* and *Hidden Documents Continued (Xu zang shu)*. The stories with Liu Ji's introductions that are translated in the present volume are drawn from *Extraordinary Strategies in a Hundred Battles (Bai-zhan qilue)*, evidently the most popular of Liu's many literary works. The excerpt from his work *The Cultured One* is from Liu's *Youlizi*. Liu's poems are translated from *Chengyibo wen-shu*. For background on Zhuge Liang I used *Records of the Three Kingdoms (Sanguo zhi)*, a court history of that era; *Tales of the Three Kingdoms (Sanguo yanyi)*, a much later historical novel about the civil wars of the time, written from a very different point of view than the court history on which it is based; and *Works by and about the Loyal Lord at Arms (Zhongwuhou ji)*, a study of Zhuge Liang found in the Taoist canon. The translations from Zhuge's writings contained in this volume are taken from collections of his essays, letters, and poetry included verbatim in the aforementioned study of his life and work in the Taoist canon.

Besides Sun Tzu's *The Art of War*, Liu Ji also quotes the following sources for his rules of battle:

"Book of the Latter Han Dynasty" (*Houhan shu*)
"Dialogues of Li, Lord of Wei" (*Li Weigong wenda*)
"Sima's Rules" or "Sima's Art of War" (*Sima bingfa*)
"Six Secrets" (*Liutao*)
"Three Strategies" (*Sanlue*)
"Zuo Family Tradition on the Spring and Autumn Annals"
   (*Zuochuan*)

PART ONE

THE WAY OF THE GENERAL

ESSAYS ON LEADERSHIP AND CRISIS MANAGEMENT

BY ZHUGE LIANG

TRANSLATOR'S
INTRODUCTION

Zhuge Liang, commonly known by his style, Kongming, was born around the year 180, the son of a provincial official in the latter days of the Han dynasty. At that time, the dynasty was thoroughly decrepit, nearly four hundred years old and on the verge of collapse. For most of his adult life, Zhuge was to play a major role in the power struggles and civil wars that followed the demise of the ancient Han.

Orphaned at an early age, he and his younger brother were taken in by an uncle, a local governor in southern China. When this uncle was replaced with another officer, he and his charges went to join an old family friend, a member of the powerful Liu clan who was currently a governor in central China. The imperial house of Han was a branch of the greater Liu clan, which as a whole retained considerable wealth, prestige, and influence even after the passing of the Han dynasty itself.

Zhuge Liang's uncle died during his sojourn in central China. Then in his twenties, Zhuge stayed there, supporting himself by farming. According to *Records of the Three Kingdoms*, at this early age Zhuge was aware of his own genius, but few took him seriously; he was, after all, an orphan and subsistence farmer. His fortunes took a turn, however, when the great warrior Liu Bei, founder of the kingdom of Shu in western China, garrisoned in the area where Zhuge Liang was living.

Zhuge was recommended to the warrior chief by a member of the influential Xu clan, which produced many outstanding Taoists of the early churches. According to *Records of the Three Kingdoms*, Zhuge's friend said to Liu Bei, "Zhuge Kongming is a dragon in repose—would you want to meet him?"

Liu Bei said, "You come with him."

The friend said, "It is possible to go see this man, but you cannot make him come to you. You, General, should go out of your way to look in on him."

The record states that Liu Bei finally went to see Zhuge Liang, adding that he had to go no fewer than three times before the young genius agreed to meet the warrior chieftain. When at length they were together, the record continues, Liu Bei dismissed everyone else so that he could be alone with Zhuge Liang. Then he said, "The house of Han is collapsing; treacherous officials are usurping authority; the emperor is blinded by the dust." The warlord went on to solicit Zhuge's advice, and Zhuge became one of his top strategists. The story of this famous meeting is related in the first of Liu Ji's war tales.

The intrigues of the era of the Three Kingdoms are too complex to detail here; indeed, they fill the one hundred chapters of the massive neoclassic historical novel *Tales of the Three Kingdoms*. Suffice it to say here that the time was one of constant turmoil, tension, and strife. In the midst of unending warfare among the three kingdoms, Zhuge Liang was appointed to positions of highest responsibility in both civil and military leadership.

When Liu Bei died, his heir was still young, so Zhuge Liang also served as the de facto regent for the new king as well as a top general and strategist. He never fell in battle, but he did die on a campaign, garrisoned in the field. Carrying burdens enough to kill two men, Zhuge Liang succumbed to illness at the age of fifty-four. Immortalized in literature for his intelligence and humanity, he was greatly admired as a warrior and administrator. His last will and testament, addressed to the young ruler of Shu, illustrates the thought and character of this remarkable individual:

> It seems to me that I am a simpleton by nature. Having run into the troubles of the times, I mobilized an army on an expedition north. Before being able to achieve complete success, I unexpectedly became mortally ill, and now I am on the brink of death.
>
> I humbly pray that the ruler will purify his heart, minimize his desires, restrain himself and love the com-

mon people, convey respect to the former ruler, spread humaneness through the land, promote conscientious individualists in order to get wise and good people into positions of responsibility, and throw out traitors and calumniators in order to make the manners of the people more substantial.

I have eight hundred mulberry trees and eight acres of thin fields, so my children and grandchildren are self-sufficient in food and clothing. I am abroad, without any particular accoutrements; I wear government-issue clothing and eat government-issue food, and do not have any other source of income for my personal use. When I die, do not let there be any extra cotton on the corpse, or any special burial objects, for which I would be indebted to the nation.

As this testament shows, there is a strong undercurrent of Taoist thought in Zhuge Liang's attitudes toward life and work. This undercurrent is even more evident in his letters of advice to his nephew and his son. To his nephew he wrote:

Aspirations should remain lofty and far-sighted. Look to the precedents of the wise. Detach from emotions and desires; get rid of any fixations. Elevate subtle feelings to presence of mind and sympathetic sense. Be patient in tight situations as well as easy ones; eliminate all pettiness.

Seek knowledge by questioning widely; set aside aversion and reluctance. What loss is there in dignity, what worry is there of failure?

If your will is not strong, if your thought does not oppose injustice, you will fritter away your life stuck in the commonplace, silently submitting to the bonds of emotion, forever cowering before mediocrities, never escaping the downward flow.

To his son, he gave this advice:

The practice of a cultivated man is to refine himself by quietude and develop virtue by frugality. Without detachment, there is no way to clarify the will; without serenity, there is no way to get far.

Study requires calm, talent requires study. Without study there is no way to expand talent; without calm there is no way to accomplish study.

If you are lazy, you cannot do thorough research; if you are impulsive, you cannot govern your nature.

The years run off with the hours, aspirations flee with the years. Eventually one ages and collapses. What good will it do to lament over poverty?

Finally, Zhuge's own motto illustrates a central quality for which he is especially honored, the quality of sincerity. Zhuge's honesty and integrity in public and private life are legendary, and his writings on social and political organization show that he considered sincerity fundamental to success in these domains. He formulated the rule of his life in this motto:

Opportunistic relationships can hardly be kept constant. The acquaintance of honorable people, even at a distance, does not add flowers in times of warmth and does not change its leaves in times of cold: it continues unfading through the four seasons, becomes increasingly stable as it passes through ease and danger.

The following essays on leadership and organization are taken from a collection of works by and about Zhuge Liang, *Records of the Loyal Lord of Warriors*, as preserved in the Taoist canon.

THE WAY OF THE GENERAL

The Authority of the Military Leadership

Military authority, directing the armed forces, is a matter of the authoritative power of the leading general.

If the general can hold the authority of the military and operate its power, he oversees his subordinates like a fierce tiger with wings, flying over the four seas, going into action whenever there is an encounter.

If the general loses his authority and cannot control the power, he is like a dragon cast into a lake; he may seek the freedom of the high seas, but how can he get there?

Chasing Evils

There are five types of harm in decadence among national armed forces.

First is the formation of factions that band together for character assassination, criticizing and vilifying the wise and the good.

Second is luxury in uniforms.

Third is wild tales and confabulations about the supernatural.

Fourth is judgment based on private views, mobilizing groups for personal reasons.

Fifth is making secret alliances with enemies, watching for where the advantage may lie.

All people like this are treacherous and immoral. You should distance yourself from them and not associate with them.

Knowing People

Nothing is harder to see into than people's natures. Though good and bad are different, their conditions and appearances are not always uniform. There are some people who are nice enough but steal. Some people are outwardly respectful while inwardly making fools of everyone. Some people are brave on the outside yet cowardly on the inside. Some people do their best but are not loyal.

Hard though it be to know people, there are ways.

First is to question them concerning right and wrong, to observe their ideas.

Second is to exhaust all their arguments, to see how they change.

Third is to consult with them about strategy, to see how perceptive they are.

Fourth is to announce that there is trouble, to see how brave they are.

Fifth is to get them drunk, to observe their nature.

Sixth is to present them with the prospect of gain, to see how modest they are.

Seventh is to give them a task to do within a specific time, to see how trustworthy they are.

Types of Generals

There are nine types of generals.

Those who guide with virtue, who treat all equally with courtesy, who know when the troops are cold and hungry, and who notice when they are weary and pained, are called humanistic generals.

Those who do not try to avoid any task, who are not influenced by profit, who would die with honor before living in disgrace, are called dutiful generals.

Those who are not arrogant because of their high status, who do not make much of their victories, who are wise but can humble themselves, who are strong but can be tolerant, are called courteous generals.

Those whose extraordinary shifts are unfathomable, whose movements and responses are multifaceted, who turn disaster into fortune and seize victory from the jaws of danger, are called clever generals.

Those who give rich rewards for going ahead and have strict penalties for retreating, whose rewards are given right away and whose penalties are the same for all ranks, even the highest, are called trustworthy generals.

Those who go on foot or on a war-horse, with the mettle to take on a hundred men, who are skilled in the use of close-range weapons, swords, and spears, are called infantry generals.

Those who face the dizzying heights and cross the dangerous defiles, who can shoot at a gallop as if in flight, who are in the vanguard when advancing and in the rear guard when withdrawing, are called cavalry generals.

Those whose mettle makes the armies tremble and whose determination makes light of powerful enemies, who are hesitant to engage in petty fights while courageous in the midst of major battles, are called fierce generals.

Those who consider themselves lacking when they see the wise, who go along with good advice like following a current, who are magnanimous yet able to be firm, who are uncomplicated yet have many strategies, are called great generals.

Capacities of Commanders

The capacities of commanders are not the same; some are greater, some are lesser.

One who spies out treachery and disaster, who wins the allegiance of others, is the leader of ten men.

One who rises early in the morning and retires late at night, and whose words are discreet yet perceptive, is the leader of a hundred men.

One who is direct yet circumspect, who is brave and can fight, is the leader of a thousand men.

One of martial bearing and fierceness of heart, who knows the hardships of others and spares people from hunger and cold, is the leader of ten thousand men.

One who associates with the wise and promotes the able, who is careful of how he spends each day, who is sincere, trustworthy, and magnanimous, and who is guarded in times of order as well as times of disturbance, is the leader of a hundred thousand men.

One whose humanitarian care extends to all under his command, whose trustworthiness and justice win the allegiance of neighboring nations, who understands the signs of the sky above, the patterns of the earth below, and the affairs of humanity in between, and who regards all people as his family, is a world-class leader, one who cannot be opposed.

Decadence in Generals

There are eight kinds of decadence in generalship.

First is to be insatiably greedy.

Second is to be jealous and envious of the wise and able.

Third is to believe slanderers and make friends with the treacherous.

Fourth is to assess others without assessing oneself.

Fifth is to be hesitant and indecisive.

Sixth is to be heavily addicted to wine and sex.

Seventh is to be a malicious liar with a cowardly heart.

Eighth is to talk wildly, without courtesy.

Loyalty in Generals

"Weapons are instruments of ill omen"; generalship is a dangerous job. Therefore if one is inflexible there will be breakdowns, and when the job is important there will be danger.

This is why a good general does not rely or presume on strength or power. He is not pleased by favor and does not fear vilification. He does not crave whatever material goods he sees, and he does not rape whatever women he can. His only intention is to pursue the best interests of the country.

Skills of Generals

There are five skills and four desires involved in generalship.

The five skills are: skill in knowing the disposition and power of enemies, skill in knowing the ways to advance and withdraw, skill in knowing how empty or how full countries are, skill in knowing nature's timing and human affairs, and skill in knowing the features of terrain.

The four desires are: desire for the extraordinary and unexpected in strategy, desire for thoroughness in security, desire for calm among the masses, and desire for unity of hearts and minds.

Arrogance in Generals

Generals should not be arrogant, for if they are arrogant they will become discourteous, and if they are discourteous people will become alienated from them. When people are alienated, they become rebellious.

Generals should not be stingy, for if they are stingy they will not reward the trustworthy, and if they do not reward the trustworthy, the soldiers will not be dedicated. If the soldiers are not dedicated, the armed forces are ineffective, and if the armed forces are ineffective, the nation is empty. When a nation is empty, its opponents are full.

Confucius said, "People may have the finest talents, but if they are arrogant and stingy, their other qualities are not worthy of consideration."

Military Preparedness

Military preparedness is the greatest task of the nation. A small mistake can make a huge difference. When the force of momentum by which soldiers are killed and generals are captured can move with sudden rapidity, should we not be wary?

Therefore when a nation is in trouble, the ruler and ministers urgently work on strategy, selecting the wise and assessing the able to delegate responsibilities to them.

If you count on safety and do not think of danger, if you do not know enough to be wary when enemies arrive, this is called a sparrow nesting on a tent, a fish swimming in a cauldron—they won't last the day.

Traditions say, "Without preparation, military operations are unfeasible."

"Preparedness against the unexpected is a way of good government."

"Even bees have venom—how much the more do nations. If you are unprepared, even if there are many of you, mere numbers cannot be counted on."

A classic document says, "Only when we do our tasks are we prepared; when we are prepared, there is no trouble."

Therefore the action of the military forces must have preparation.

Training

Soldiers without training cannot stand up to one out of a hundred opponents, yet they are sent out against a hundred each. This is why Confucius said, "To send people to war without teaching them is called abandoning them." It is also said, "Teach the people for seven years, and they too can go to war."

Therefore soldiers must be taught without fail. First train them in conduct and duty, teach them to be loyal and trustworthy, instruct them in rules and penalties, awe them with rewards and punishments. When people know enough to follow along, then train them in maneuvers.

One person can teach ten, ten people can teach a hundred, a hundred people can teach a thousand, a thousand can teach ten thousand, thus developing the armed forces. Train like this, and opponents will surely lose.

Corruption in the Armed Forces

In military operations it may happen that scouts are not careful of their signal fires; or there may be mistakes in calculation and consequent delays, infractions of rules, failure to respond to the time and situation, disorder in the ranks, callous and unreasonable demands made by superiors on their subordinates, pursuit of self-interest, lack of concern for the hungry and cold, tall tales and fortune telling, rabble rousing, confusing the officers, refusal of the mettlesome to submit to authority, contempt of superiors, or using supplies for personal enjoyment. These things corrupt the armed forces. When they are present, there is certain to be defeat.

Loyal Hearts

Those who would be military leaders must have loyal hearts, eyes and ears, claws and fangs. Without people loyal to them, they are like someone walking at night, not knowing where to step. Without eyes and ears, they are as though in the dark, not knowing how to proceed. Without claws and fangs, they are like hungry men eating poisoned food, inevitably to die.

Therefore good generals always have intelligent and learned associates for their advisors, thoughtful and careful associates for their eyes and ears, brave and formidable associates for their claws and fangs.

Careful Watching

The loss of an army is always caused by underestimating an opponent and thus bringing on disaster. Therefore an army goes out in an orderly manner. If order is lost, that bodes ill.

There are fifteen avenues of order:

1. Thoughtfulness, using secret agents for intelligence
2. Organization, gathering news and watching carefully
3. Courage, not being disturbed by the number of the enemy
4. Modesty, thinking of justice and duty when seeing the opportunity for gain
5. Impartiality, being egalitarian in matters of rewards and punishments
6. Forbearance, being able to bear humiliation
7. Magnanimity, being able to accept the masses
8. Trustworthiness, so that there can be serious cooperation
9. Respect, honoring the wise and able
10. Clarity of mind, not listening to slander
11. Reason, not forgetting past experience
12. Human kindness, taking care of the soldiers
13. Loyalty, devoting oneself to the nation
14. Moderation, knowing to stop when you have enough of anything
15. Planning, assessing yourself first, and then assessing others

Formation of Opportunity

To overcome the intelligent by folly is contrary to the natural order of things; to overcome the foolish by intelligence is in accord with the natural order. To overcome the intelligent by intelligence, however, is a matter of opportunity.

There are three avenues of opportunity: events, trends, and conditions. When opportunities occur through events but you are unable to respond, you are not smart. When opportunities become active through a trend and yet you cannot make plans, you are not wise. When opportunities emerge through conditions but you cannot act on them, you are not bold.

Those skilled in generalship always achieve their victories by taking advantage of opportunities.

Good Generalship

Good generals of ancient times had some overall principles:

1. Show people when to proceed and when to withdraw, and people will learn regulation.
2. Array them on the lines rightly and justly, and people will be orderly.
3. Show respect for them by your judgments, and people will be enthusiastic.
4. Motivate them with rewards and penalties, and people will be trusting.

Regulation, order, enthusiasm, and trust are the overall principles of generals, by which they are able to ensure victory in battle.

The mediocre are not like this: they cannot stop their troops when they retreat, they cannot control their troops when they advance, they mix up good and bad, the soldiers are not given instruction and encouragement, rewards and punishments are not fair. Because people are not trusting, the wise and the good withdraw, while flatterers are promoted. Such an army will therefore inevitably be defeated in war.

Discerning Bases

If you attack evils based on social trends, no one can rival you in dignity. If you settle victory based on the power of the people, no one can rival you in achievement.

If you can accurately discern these bases of action, and add dignity and faith to them, you can take on the most formidable opponent and prevail over the most valiant adversary.

Victory and Defeat

When the wise and talented are in the higher positions and undesirables are in low positions, the armed forces are happy. When the soldiers are scared, if they talk to each other of valiant combat, look to each other for martial dignity, and urge each other on by rewards and penalties, these are signs of certain victory.

When the armies have been shaken up several times, if the soldiers become lazy, insubordinate, untrustworthy, and unruly, if they scare each other with talk about the enemy, if they talk to each other about booty, make hints to each other of disaster and fortune, or confuse each other with weird talk, these are signs of certain defeat.

Using Authority

People's lives depend on generals, as do success and failure, calamity and fortune; so if the rulership does not give them the power to reward and punish, this is like tying up a monkey and trying to make it cavort around, or like gluing someone's eyes shut and asking him to distinguish colors.

If rewards are up to powerful civilians and punishments do not come from the generals, people will seek personal profit— then who will have any interest in fighting? Even with superlative strategy and performance, self-defense would be impossible under these circumstances.

Therefore Sun Tzu the Martialist said, "When a general is in the field, there are some orders he doesn't accept from the civilian ruler." It is also said, "In the army, you hear the orders of the generals, you don't hear about commands from the emperor."

Grieving for the Dead

Good generals of ancient times took care of their people as one might take care of a beloved child. When there was difficulty they would face it first themselves, and when something was achieved they would defer to others. They would tearfully console the wounded and sorrowfully mourn the dead. They would sacrifice themselves to feed the hungry and remove their own garments to clothe the cold. They honored the wise and provided for their living; they rewarded and encouraged the brave. If generals can be like this, they can take over anywhere they go.

Allies

To operate, the armed forces need allies as consultants and assistants to the leadership.

Everyone looks up to those who are thoughtful and have unusual strategies beyond the ordinary ken, who are widely learned and have broad vision, and who have many skills and great talents. Such people can be made top allies.

Those who are fierce, swift, firm, and sharp are heroes of an age. Such people can be made second-ranked allies.

Those who talk a lot but not always to the point, who are slight in ability, with little that is extraordinary, are people with ordinary capabilities. They can be brought along as the lower class of allies.

Responsiveness

When you plan for difficulty in times of ease, when you do the great while it is still small, when you use rewards first and penalties later, this is refinement in use of the military.

When the troops are already on the battlefield, the cavalries are charging each other, the catapults have been set in position, and the infantries meet at close range, if you can use awesome authoritativeness to convey a sense of trust such that opponents surrender, this is ability in use of the military.

If you plunge into a hail of arrows and rocks, facing off in a contest for victory, with winning and losing distinct, if your adversary is wounded but you die, this is inferiority in use of the military.

Taking Opportunities

The art of certain victory, the mode of harmonizing with changes, is a matter of opportunity. Who but the perspicacious can deal with it? And of all avenues of seeing opportunity, none is greater than the unexpected.

Assessing Abilities

Those who employed warriors skillfully in ancient times assessed their abilities in order to calculate the prospects of victory or defeat:

Who has the wiser ruler?
Who has the more intelligent generals?
Who has the more able officers?

Whose food supplies are most abundant?
Whose soldiers are better trained?
Whose legions are more orderly?
Whose war-horses are swifter?
Whose formations and situation are more dangerous?
Whose clients and allies are smarter?
Whose neighbors are more frightened?
Who has more goods and money?
Whose citizenry is calmer?

When you consider matters along these lines, structural strengths and weaknesses can be determined.

Facilitating Battle

A scorpion will sting because it has poison; a soldier can be brave when he can rely on his equipment. Therefore when their weapons are sharp and their armor is strong, people will readily do battle. If armor is not strong, it is the same as baring one's shoulders. If a bow cannot shoot far, it is the same as a close-range weapon. If a shot cannot hit the mark, it is the same as having no weapon. If a scout is not careful, it is the same as having no eyes. If a general is not brave in battle, it is the same as having no military leadership.

Striking Power

Skilled warriors of ancient times first found out the condition of their enemies, and then made plans to deal with them. There is no doubt of success when you strike enemies under the following conditions:

Their fighting forces are stale.
Their supplies are exhausted.
Their populace is full of sorrow and bitterness.
Many people are physically ill.
They do not plan ahead.
Their equipment is in disrepair.
Their soldiers are not trained.
Reinforcements do not show up.
Night falls when they still have a long way to go.
Their soldiers are worn out.

Their generals are contemptuous and their officers inconsiderate.

They neglect to make preparations.

They do not form battle lines as they advance.

When they do form battle lines, they are not stable.

They are disorderly when they travel over rough terrain.

There is discord between commanders and soldiers.

They become arrogant when they win a battle.

There is disorder in the ranks when they move their battle lines.

The soldiers are tired and prone to upset.

The army is supplied, but the people do not eat.

Each man moves on his own—some go ahead, some lag behind.

When opponents have the following qualities, however, withdraw and avoid them:

Superiors are considerate and subordinates are obedient.

Rewards are sure and punishments certain.

The forces are set out in an orderly fashion.

They give responsibility to the wise and employ the able.

The army is courteous and mannerly.

Their armor is strong and their weapons keen.

They have plenty of supplies and equipment.

Their government and education are substantial.

They are on good terms with all of their neighbors.

They are backed by great nations.

Psychological Configurations

Some generals are brave and think lightly of death. Some are hasty and impulsive. Some are greedy and materialistic. Some are humane but lack endurance. Some are intelligent but timid. Some are intelligent but easygoing at heart.

Those who are brave and think lightly of death are vulnerable to assault. Those who are hasty and impulsive are vulnerable to delay. Those who are greedy and materialistic are vulnerable to loss. Those who are humane but lack endurance are vulnerable to fatigue. Those who are intelligent but timid are vulnerable to pressure. Those who are intelligent but easygoing are vulnerable to sudden attack.

Orderly Troops

In military operations, order leads to victory. If rewards and penalties are unclear, if rules and regulations are unreliable, and if signals are not followed, even if you have an army of a million strong it is of no practical benefit.

An orderly army is one that is mannerly and dignified, one that cannot be withstood when it advances and cannot be pursued when it withdraws. Its movements are regulated and directed; this gives it security and presents no danger. The troops can be massed but not scattered, can be deployed but not worn out.

Inspiring Soldiers

Honor them with titles, present them with goods, and soldiers willingly come join you. Treat them courteously, inspire them with speeches, and soldiers willingly die. Give them nourishment and rest so that they do not become weary, make the code of rules uniform, and soldiers willingly obey. Lead them into battle personally, and soldiers will be brave. Record even a little good, reward even a little merit, and soldiers will be encouraged.

Self-Exertion

Sages follow the rules of heaven; the wise obey the laws of earth; the intelligent follow precedent. Harm comes to the arrogant; calamity visits the proud. Few people trust those who talk too much; few people feel indebted to the self-serving. Rewarding the unworthy causes alienation; punishing the innocent causes resentment. Those whose appreciation or anger are unpredictable perish.

Harmonizing People

Harmonizing people is essential in military operations. When people are in harmony, they will fight on their own initiative, without exhortation. If the officers and the soldiers are suspi-

cious of one another, then warriors will not join up. If no heed
is paid to the strategies of the loyal, then small-minded people
will backbite. When the sprouts of hypocrisy arise, even if you
have the wisdom of the great warrior-kings of old, you will not
be able to prevail over an ordinary man, much less a whole
group of them. Therefore tradition says, "A military operation
is like fire; if it is not stopped, it burns itself out."

The Condition of a General

According to the code of generalship, generals do not say they
are thirsty before the soldiers have drawn from the well; generals
do not say they are hungry before the soldiers' food is cooked;
generals do not say they are cold before the soldiers' fires are
kindled; generals do not say they are hot before the soldiers'
canopies are drawn. Generals do not use fans in summer, do
not wear leather in winter, do not use umbrellas in the rain.
They do as everyone does.

Order and Disorder

When a nation is perilous and disorderly, and the people are
not secure in their homes, this is because the ruler has made
the mistake of neglecting to find wise people.

When the wise are disaffected, a nation is in peril; when
the wise are employed, a nation is secure. When offices are
chosen for persons, there is disorder; when persons are chosen
for offices, there is order.

Observant Government

An observant and perceptive government is one that looks at
subtle phenomena and listens to small voices. When phenomena are subtle they are not seen, and when voices are small
they are not heard; therefore an enlightened leader looks closely
at the subtle and listens for the importance of the small voice.

This harmonizes the outside with the inside, and harmonizes the inside with the outside; so the Way of government
involves the effort to see and hear much.

Thus when you are alert to what the people in the lower
echelons have to say, and take it into consideration, so that

your plans include the rank and file, then all people are your eyes and a multitude of voices helps your ears. This is the reason for the classic saying, "A sage has no constant mind— the people are the sage's mind."

Rulers and Ministers

For rulers, generosity to subordinates is benevolence; for ministers, service of the government is duty. No one should serve the government with duplicity; ministers should not be given dubious policies.

When both superiors and subordinates are given to courtesy, then the people are easy to employ. When superiors and subordinates are in harmony, then the Way of rulers and ministers is fulfilled: rulers employ their ministers courteously, while ministers work for the rulers loyally; rulers plan the government policies, while ministers plan their implementation.

Knowledgeable Rule

Rulers are considered knowledgeable according to how much they have seen, and are considered capable according to how much they have heard.

Everyone knows the saying that an intelligent ruler is constant through the day and night, discharging the affairs of office by day and attending to personal matters at night. Yet there may be grievances that do not get a hearing, and there may be loyal people promoting good who are not trusted.

If grievances are not heard, the bent cannot be straightened. If promotion of good is not accepted, the loyal are not trusted and the treacherous enter with their schemes.

This is the meaning of the proverb in the ancient "Classic of Documents": "Heaven sees through the seeing of my people, heaven hears through the hearing of my people."

Not Knowing

Confucius said that an enlightened ruler does not worry about people not knowing him, he worries about not knowing people. He worries not about outsiders not knowing insiders, but about insiders not knowing outsiders. He worries not about subordinates not knowing superiors, but about superiors not knowing subordinates. He worries not about the lower classes not knowing the upper classes, but about the upper classes not knowing the lower classes.

Adjudication

When rulers adjudicate criminal cases and execute punishments, they worry that they may be unclear. The innocent may be punished while the guilty may be released. The powerful may arrogate to themselves alone the right to speak, while the powerless may have their rights infringed upon by those who bear grudges against them. Honesty may be distorted; those who are wronged may not get a chance to express themselves. The trustworthy may be suspected; the loyal may be attacked. These are all perversions, problems causing disaster and violence, aberrations causing calamity and chaos.

Disturbance and Security

It is said that when officials are severe in everything, no one knows where it will end. If they feed off the people so severely that people are hungry and impoverished, this produces disturbance and rebellion.

Encourage people in productive work, don't deprive them of their time. Lighten their taxes, don't exhaust their resources. In this way the country is made wealthy and families secure.

Appointments

The official policy of making appointments should be to promote the upright and place them over the crooked. Governing a country is like governing the body. The way to govern the body is to nurture the spirit; the way to govern a country is to promote the wise. Life is sought by nurturing the spirit; stability is sought by promoting the wise.

So public servants are to a nation as pillars are to a house: the pillars should not be slender; public servants should not be weak. When pillars are slender the house collapses; when public servants are weak the nation crumbles. Therefore the way to govern a nation is to promote the upright over the crooked; then the nation is secure.

Pillars of State

For strong pillars you need straight trees; for wise public servants you need upright people. Straight trees are found in remote forests; upright people come from the humble masses. Therefore when rulers are going to make appointments they need to look in obscure places.

Sometimes there are disenfranchised people with something of value in them; sometimes there are people with extraordinary talent who go unrecognized. Sometimes there are paragons of virtue who are not promoted by their hometowns; sometimes there are people who live in obscurity on purpose.

Sometimes there are people who are dutiful and righteous for purely philosophical or religious reasons. Sometimes there are loyal people who are straightforward with rulers but are slandered by cliques. Ancient kings are known to have hired unknowns and nobodies, finding in them the human qualities whereby they were able to bring peace.

Evaluation and Dismissal

The official policy of evaluation and dismissal should be to promote the good and dismiss the bad. An enlightened leadership is aware of good and bad throughout the realm, not daring to overlook even minor officials and commoners, employing the wise and good, and dismissing the greedy and weak-minded.

With enlightened leadership and good citizens, projects get accomplished, the nation is orderly, and the wise gather like rain; this is the way to promote the good and dismiss the bad, setting forth what is acceptable and what is blameworthy. Therefore a policy of evaluation and dismissal means effort to know what hurts the people.

What Hurts the People

There are five things that hurt the people:

1. There are local officials who use public office for personal benefit, taking improper advantage of their authority, holding weapons in one hand and people's livelihood in the other, corrupting their offices, and bleeding the people.
2. There are cases where serious offenses are given light

penalties; there is inequality before the law, and the innocent are subjected to punishment, even execution. Sometimes serious crimes are pardoned, the strong are supported, and the weak are oppressed. Harsh penalties are applied, unjustly torturing people to get at facts.

3. Sometimes there are officials who condone crime and vice, punishing those who protest against this, cutting off the avenues of appeal and hiding the truth, plundering and ruining lives, unjust and arbitrary.

4. Sometimes there are senior officials who repeatedly change department heads so as to monopolize the government administration, favoring their friends and relatives while treating those they dislike with unjust harshness, oppressive in their actions, prejudiced and unruly. They also use taxation to reap profit, enriching themselves and their families by exactions and fraud.

5. Sometimes local officials extensively tailor awards and fines, welfare projects, and general expenditures, arbitrarily determining prices and measures, with the result that people lose their jobs.

These five things are harmful to the people, and anyone who does any of these should be dismissed from office.

Military Action

"Weapons are instruments of ill omen, to be used only when it is unavoidable." The proper course of military action is to establish strategy first, and then carry it out. Monitor the environment, observe the minds of the masses, practice the use of military equipment, clarify the principles of reward and punishment, watch the schemes of enemies, note the perils of the roads, distinguish safe and dangerous places, find out the conditions of the parties involved, and recognize when to proceed and when to withdraw. Follow the timing of opportunities, set up preparations for defense, strengthen your striking power, improve the abilities of your soldiers, map out decisive strategies, and consider life and death issues. Only after doing all this should you send out armed forces, appointing military leaders and extending the power to capture enemies. This is the overall scheme of things in military matters.

Rewards and Penalties

A policy of rewards and penalties means rewarding the good and penalizing wrongdoers. Rewarding the good is to promote achievement; penalizing wrongdoers is to prevent treachery.

It is imperative that rewards and punishments be fair and impartial. When they know rewards are to be given, courageous warriors know what they are dying for; when they know penalties are to be applied, villains know what to fear.

Therefore, rewards should not be given without reason, and penalties should not be applied arbitrarily. If rewards are given for no reason, those who have worked hard in public service will be resentful; if penalties are applied arbitrarily, upright people will be bitter.

Clarity and Consistency

Generals hold authority over life and death. If they allow those who should live to be killed, or allow those who should be killed to live, or if they get angry without discernible reason, or their punishments and rewards are not clear, or commands are inconsistent, or they carry their private affairs over into public life, this is dangerous for the nation.

If their punishments and rewards are not clear, their directives will not always be followed. If they allow those who should be killed to live, treachery will not be prevented. If they allow those who should live to be killed, soldiers will defect. If they get angry without discernible reason, their authority will not be effective. If their rewards and punishments are not clear, the lower echelons will not be encouraged to achieve. If policies are inappropriate, orders will not be obeyed. If private affairs are carried over into public life, people will be of two minds.

If treachery is not prevented, it is impossible to last long. If soldiers defect, the ranks will be decimated. If authority is ineffective, the troops will not rise up in the face of the enemy. If the lower echelons are not encouraged to achieve, the upper echelons have no strong support. If orders are not obeyed, affairs will be chaotic. If people are of two minds, the country will be in danger.

Pleasure and Displeasure

Displeasure should not lead you to harm people who have done no wrong; pleasure should not lead you to go along with those who deserve to be executed.

Pleasure should not induce you to forgive those who have done wrong; displeasure should not induce you to execute the innocent.

Pleasure and displeasure should not be arbitrary; personal prejudices ignore worthy people. A general should not start a battle out of personal displeasure; it is imperative to go by the collective will. If he does go into battle because of personal displeasure, it will certainly result in defeat.

Culture and the Military

Culture takes precedence; the military comes after. If you put victory first, you will surely get beaten later; if you start out with anger, you will surely regret it later. One day's anger can destroy your whole life. Therefore a superior man is stern but not ferocious: he may get angry, but not furious; he may worry, but does not fear; he may rejoice, but is not overjoyed.

Organization

A policy to quell disorder involves minimizing offices and combining duties, getting rid of embellishment in favor of substance.

First organize directives, then organize penalties. First organize the near at hand, then organize the far removed. First organize the inner, then organize the outer. First organize the basic, then organize the derivative. First organize the strong, then organize the weak. First organize the great, then organize the small. First organize yourself, then organize others.

Instruction and Direction

A policy of instruction and direction means those above educate those below, not saying anything that is unlawful and not doing anything that is immoral, for what is done by those above is observed by those below.

To indulge oneself yet instruct others is contrary to proper government; to correct oneself and then teach others is in accord with proper government. Therefore true leaders first rectify themselves and only after that do they promulgate their directives. If they are not upright themselves, their directives will not be followed, resulting in disorder.

Therefore the Way of leadership puts education and direction before punishment. To send people to war without education is tantamount to throwing them away.

Thought and Consideration

A policy of thought and consideration means giving thought to what is near at hand and considering what is remote. As it is said, "If people do not consider what is remote, they will have trouble near at hand." Therefore "educated people think without leaving their positions." Thinking means correct strategy, consideration means thinking of plans for eventualities. One is not to plan policy when it is not one's place to do so, or consider the scheme of things that are none of one's business.

Major affairs arise in difficulty, minor affairs arise in ease. Therefore if you want to think of the advantages in a situation, it is imperative to consider the harm; if you want to think about success, it is imperative to consider failure.

Danger arises in safety, destruction arises in survival. Harm arises in advantage, chaos arises in order. Enlightened people know the obvious when they see the subtle, know the end when they see the beginning; thus there is no way for disaster to happen. This is due to thoughtful consideration.

Strength in Generals

Generals have five strengths and eight evils.

The five strengths are: noble behavior that can inspire the common people, social virtues that can elevate their reputations, trustworthiness and dutifulness in personal relationships, universal love encompassing all the people, and powerful action to succeed in their tasks.

The eight evils are: inability to assess right and wrong when formulating strategy, inability to delegate authority to the wise and the good in times of order, inability to mete out just punishments for incidents of disorder, inability to help the poor in times of plenty, insufficient intelligence to guard against threats before they have taken shape, insufficient thought to prevent subtle dangers, inability to express what is known intuitively, and inability to avoid criticism in defeat.

Sending Out the Armed Forces

In ancient times, when a nation was in trouble, the ruler would select a wise man and have him fast for three days in quiet seclusion before going to the gate of the national shrine, where he would stand facing south. He then took a high courtier to present a ceremonial axe to the ruler, who in turn would pass it by the handle to the general, saying:

"The military leadership settles matters outside the borders," and also directing him in these terms:

"Where you see the enemy to be empty, proceed; where you see the enemy to be full, stop.

"Do not look down on others because of your own elevated rank.

"Do not oppose the common consensus with personal opinions.

"Do not turn from the loyal and trustworthy through the artifices of the skilled but treacherous.

"Do not sit down before the soldiers sit; do not eat before the soldiers eat.

"Bear the same cold and heat the soldiers do; share their toil as well as their ease.

"Experience sweetness and bitterness just as the soldiers do; take the same risks that they do.

"Then the soldiers will exert themselves to the utmost, and it will be possible to destroy enemies."

Having accepted these words, the general led the armed forces out through the city's gate of ill omen.

The ruler, seeing the general off, knelt and said, "Advance and retreat are a matter of timing—military affairs are not directed by the ruler but by the general. Therefore 'There is no heaven above, no earth below, no adversary ahead, and no ruler behind.' Thus the intelligent think because of this; the mettlesome fight because of this."

Selection on Abilities

In military action, there are men who like to fight and enjoy battle, singlehandedly taking on powerful opponents; gather them into one squad and call them "the warriors who repay the nation."

There are mettlesome men with ability and strength, courage and speed; gather them into a squad and call them "the warriors who crash the battle lines."

There are those who are light of foot, good walkers and runners; gather them into a squad called "the warriors who capture the flag."

There are those who can shoot on horseback, swift as flight, hitting the mark every time; gather them into one squad and call them "the galloping warriors."

There are archers whose aim is accurate and deadly; gather them into one squad and call them "the warriors of the fighting edge."

There are those who can shoot heavy crossbows and catapults accurately at great distances; gather them into one squad and call them "the warriors who crush the enemy's edge."

These six kinds of skilled warriors should be employed according to their particular skills.

The Use of Knowledge

Generalship requires one to follow nature, depend on timing, and rely on people in order to achieve victory.

Therefore, if nature works but the timing doesn't work, and yet people act, this is called opposing the time.

If the timing works but nature isn't cooperating, and still people act, this is called opposing nature.

If timing and nature both work, but people do not act, this is called opposing people.

Those who know do not oppose nature, do not oppose the time, and do not oppose people.

Not Setting Up Battle Lines

In ancient times, those who governed well did not arm, and those who were armed well did not set up battle lines. Those who set up battle lines well did not fight, those who fought well did not lose, and those who lost well did not perish.

The government of the sages of old was such that people were comfortable in their homes and enjoyed their work, living to old age without ever attacking one another. "Those who govern well do not arm."

When King Shun (reigned 2255–2207 B.C.E.) organized rules and penalties for wrongdoing, he accordingly created knights, or warriors. But people did not violate the rules, and no penalties were enforced. "Those who arm well do not set up battle lines."

Later, King Yu (reigned 2205–2197 B.C.E.) made a punitive expedition against the Miao tribes, but all he did was demonstrate the martial and cultural arts, and the Miao people became more civilized. "Those who set up battle lines well do not fight."

King Tang (reigned 1766–1753 B.C.E.) and King Wu (reigned 1134–1115 B.C.E.) pledged armies for one military operation, by which the whole land was decisively pacified. "Those who fight well do not lose."

When King Zhao of Chu (reigned 515–488 B.C.E.) ran into disaster, he fled to Qin for help, and ultimately was able to get his kingdom back. "Those who lose well do not perish."

Sincerity in Generals

An ancient document says, "Those who are contemptuous of cultured people have no way to win people's hearts completely; those who are contemptuous of common people have no way to get people to work as hard as they can."

For military operations it is essential to strive to win the hearts of heroes, to make the rules of rewards and punishments strict, to include both cultural and martial arts, and to combine both hard and soft techniques.

Enjoy social amenities and music; familiarize yourself with poetry and prose. Put humanity and justice before wit and bravery.

In stillness be as quiet as a fish in the deep, in action be as swift as an otter. Dissolve enemies' collusion; break down their strengths. Dazzle people with your banners; alert people with cymbals and drums.

Withdraw like a mountain in movement, advance like a rainstorm. Strike and crush with shattering force; go into battle like a tiger.

Press enemies and contain them; lure and entice them. Confuse them and seize them; be humble to make them proud. Be familiar yet distant; weaken them by lending strength.

Give security to those in danger; gladden those in fear. If people oppose you, take what they say to heart; if people have grudges, let them express themselves.

Restrain the strong, sustain the weak. Get to know those with plans; cover up any slander. When there is booty, distribute it.

Do not count on your strength and take an opponent lightly. Do not be conceited about your abilities and think little of subordinates.

Do not let personal favor congeal into authority.

Plan before acting. Fight only when you know you can win.

Do not keep the spoils of war for your own possession and use.

If generals can be like this, people will be willing to fight when they give the orders, and the enemy will be defeated before any blood is shed.

PART TWO

LESSONS OF WAR

STUDIES IN STRATEGY

BY LIU JI

TRANSLATOR'S
INTRODUCTION

Liu Ji was born in 1311 C.E., during the Yuan dynasty. An exceptionally brilliant scholar, he earned an advanced degree in the state civil service examinations and was promoted to public office. While in office, Liu gained a reputation for integrity and honesty, but while these qualities endeared him to the local populace they made him a marked man among the ruling Mongol elite. As an alien dynasty that had to depend on the native Chinese bureaucracy, the Yuan regime was wary of close bonding between local officials and the people at large.

It had already been a long-standing policy of the Chinese government to appoint officials to posts outside of their own home areas, in order to prevent the growth of local factionalism. This in turn produced other problems, but in any event the whole syndrome of unease stemming from tension between central and regional interests naturally became aggravated under alien regimes like the Mongol Yuan. This tension is a pervasive thread of Chinese history, one that is clearly evident in the triumphs and trials of the great Liu Ji.

In 1348 Liu was appointed by the Yuan government to direct a containment action against an insurrection, for Liu was not only a brilliant scholar but also a distinguished strategist. Checked by Liu's masterful engineering, the leader of the rebellion attempted to save himself with a handsome bribe. Liu refused, so the rebel went to Peking, the Mongols' capital in China, and succeeded in bribing his way into favor there.

Now the secessionist was given an office and a stipend for his trouble, while Liu Ji's relationship with the regime deteriorated further. Eventually he retired to his ancestral homeland. Here he attracted a following without really trying to do so, as many people came to him fleeing the depredations of that same rebel leader who had bought his way directly into the Yuan government. In 1366 Liu was invited to the headquarters of Zhu Yuanzhang, onetime follower of a warrior band of radical White Lotus Buddhists, now a leader of one of the popular anti-Yuan movements rising in the south of China.

Zhu was immediately impressed by the strategic thinking of the elder Liu, who was now fifty-five and well seasoned in political and military affairs. Under Liu's able guidance, in eight years Zhu established dominance over all the other insurrectionists in the south and moved north to overthrow the Mongol usurpers. When Zhu set up the Ming dynasty, restoring native rule to China, Liu Ji was one of his most trusted advisors and made perhaps the greatest contribution to the establishment of the new order.

Liu Ji's death in 1375 at the age of sixty-four has a ring of tragic irony to it, but from another point of view it would seem to be an outcome of his heroism and his final lesson to the world. Though he was the target of envious interlopers throughout his distinguished career, Liu Ji himself was known for impartiality in his judgments; this was one reason his advice was so highly esteemed, but it also cost him his life. One of the men whose proposed appointment to high office was rejected by Liu Ji contrived to effect Liu's downfall by convincing the emperor that Liu was plotting to establish his own power base. Liu was stripped of his emolument, and the whisperer was promoted.

The shock and outrage of the event destroyed Liu's health, and he soon passed away. He had told the emperor quite honestly that it was not impossible to find good men for government if he were really sincere, but none of those the emperor had with him were worthy. In particular, he warned the emperor that the individual who was to intrigue against him was like a chariot horse that may well break its harness. As it turned out, it was the interloper, now a high official of the new Ming dynasty, and not Liu Ji, who had been scheming to establish his own power base for a coup d'état. He even formed alliances with Mongolian nobles of the defunct Yuan dynasty, hoping to overthrow the Ming. When the plot was discovered, over thirty thousand people were convicted of conspiracy. So the final lesson of Liu Ji was that half of good advice is knowing when to take it. As he said to the emperor of Ming China, "Why worry that there is no talent in the country? Just let an enlightened leadership seek it wholeheartedly."

Liu Ji is famous not only as a warrior, strategist, and statesman, but also as a poet and writer. One of his early works, entitled *The Cultured One*, written during his first retirement, illustrates his philosophy of life, society, and government. In a passage on conflict avoidance, Liu demonstrates his understanding of the Taoist attitude characteristic of the higher strategy extolled in Sun Tzu's classic *The Art of War*:

> Good warriors lessen opponents, bad warriors increase opponents. Those who decrease opponents flourish thereby, those who increase opponents perish.
>
> If you want to take other people's nations, then the people of those nations are all your opponents. Therefore those who are good at lessening opponents do not cause people to oppose them.
>
> The reason wise leaders of old had no opponents was that they used their opponents to oppose opponents. Only the most humane people in the world can use their opponents to oppose opponents; for this reason opponents did not oppose them, and everyone capitulated.

Further insights into Liu's political and practical thinking can be gleaned from his poetry. Several of his verses show his profound grasp of the contradictions of historical processes and the paradoxical strategy of *The Art of War* at its best:

> A nation does not prosper itself;
> If its people have enough, it is prosperous.
> Rulers are not powerful themselves;
> When they have many knights they are strong.
> So when those full of envy are in office,
> Knights retire to private life,
> And rulers just bleed them with taxes.
> When bureaucrats advance, people get hurt,
> And then the nation is wounded.
>
> When force brings loss of freedom,
> A little flexibility can overcome a great power.
> When there is stasis in formation,

Even the mighty and ferocious
Cannot conquer the small but secure.
Thus a man-eating tiger cannot swallow a single porcupine,
But a goat leash may be used to harness nine gelded bulls.

There are impasses and successes
As a matter of course:
One cannot prevail just by wits.
Fame may be gained or lost,
And cannot be achieved by force.
So even if you have no worldly ambitions,
You won't necessarily escape slander.
Even if you seek nothing from others,
Your advice won't necessarily be put into effect.

Those who save the world from chaos
Are not occupied with petty matters;
Those who accomplish the ongoing evolution of the world
Are not conceited over small accomplishments.
So that which cuts rotting flesh
Is not to be considered a sharp sword,
And that which penetrates a naked body
Is not to be considered a good bow.

Liu Ji's philosophy of war is epitomized in certain chapters from his neoclassic *Extraordinary Strategies of a Hundred Battles*. This book, based mainly on *The Art of War* and its congeners, is one of Liu's most famous and popular works; it is the source of the war tales translated in this volume. The following selections would seem to summarize both philosophical and strategic mainstays of his thinking on conflict management, showing his intimate connection with classic traditions:

Forgetting about Warfare

Sages are very careful not to forget about danger when secure, not to forget about chaos in times of order. Even when there is peace in the land, it will not do to abandon the military altogether. If you lack sufficient foresight, you will be defenseless. It is necessary to develop cultured qualities internally while organizing military preparedness externally. Be considerate and gentle toward foreigners, beware of the unexpected. Routine military exercises in each of the four seasons is the way to show that the nation is not oblivious to warfare. Not forgetting about warfare means teaching the people not to give up the practice of martial arts.

The rule is "Even if the land is at peace, to forget about warfare leads to collapse."

Caution in War

In warfare, you should remain cautious. Go into action only when you see that it will be advantageous; if you see no advantage, then stop. Be prudent and do not act too readily. Then you will not fall into deadly situations.

The rule is "Be immovable as a mountain."

Relaxation

In war, you should not relax when you have scored a victory. You should be even more strictly on guard against enemies, still diligent even while at ease.

The rule is "Be prepared, and you will have no trouble."

Security

When enemies come from far off at the peak of their energy, it is to their advantage to fight right away; so increase your defenses, preserve your security, and do not respond—wait for them to wind down. Even if they try something to agitate you and pick a fight, do not move.

The rule is "Be still when in a secure place."

Change

The essence of the principles of warriors is responding to changes; expertise is a matter of knowing the military. In any action it is imperative to assess the enemy first. If opponents show no change or movement, then wait for them. Take advantage of change to respond accordingly, and you will benefit.

The rule is "The ability to gain victory by changing and adapting according to opponents is called genius."

Militarism

Weapons are instruments of ill omen, war is immoral. Really they are only to be resorted to when there is no other choice. It is not right to pursue aggressive warfare because one's country is large and prosperous, for this ultimately ends in defeat and destruction. Then it is too late to have regrets. Military action is like a fire—if not stopped it will burn itself out. Military expansion and adventurism soon lead to disaster.

The rule is "Even if a country is large, if it is militaristic it will eventually perish."

Like the works of all the great philosophers of the East, Liu Ji's stories of strategy are primarily aimed at stimulating thought and analyzing situations. Even while example and anecdote are commonly used in the presentations of the classical thinkers, the questions of when and how to apply principles are by nature open. Confucius said, "If I bring up one corner and you cannot come back with the other three, I won't talk to you anymore." Symbolically, this famous statement is understood to mean that practical philosophy yields relatively little without context and reflection.

Because these tales from Chinese history are stories of war, there is horror in them. As an editor, Liu Ji does not say what should happen from an ethical point of view but observes what can and does happen to human thinking and behavior in the event of contention and conflict. On one level, the stories are meant to be viewed with detachment, as a method of understanding human behavior objectively. On another level, even the sensationalism of this horror is originally didactic, fortifying the traditional moral repulsion from warfare with direct emotional and physical repulsion. Nevertheless, in the final analysis the rational and ethical ingredients in the use of these tales on the art of war are inevitably supplied by the individual who uses them, even if only by default. According to legend, when Solomon was offered wisdom or riches, he chose wisdom and was granted riches as well.

CHRONOLOGY OF HISTORICAL PERIODS
IN LIU JI'S TALES

Spring and Autumn Era (722–481 B.C.E.)
This era is generally cited to mark early to middle stages of the deterioration of the classical Zhou dynasty and the beginnings

of militarism. Confucius lived in the last century of this period. The Taoist classic *Tao Te Ching* is also popularly believed to have been compiled around the end of this era.

Warring States Era (480–246 B.C.E.)

A period of prolonged civil war among the various states of the old confederation under the titular head of the Zhou dynasty. The Warring States era is generally cited to mark middle to late stages of the degeneration and demise of the Zhou dynasty. A great deal of classical literature from various schools dates from this period, including the works of Mozi and Mencius as well as *The Art of War*.

The Qin Dynasty (246–206 B.C.E.)

The first imperial dynasty, destroying the old system of feudal states in favor of uniform law administered by a central government. The name Qin (pronounced like the English word *chin*) would seem to be the root of the English word *China*, which bears no relation to what the Chinese call themselves. Bringing the Warring States era to a close and unifying China politically and culturally, the Qin dynasty was short but eventful.

The Han Dynasty (206 B.C.E.–220 C.E.)

Under the wasteful and cruel regime of the second emperor of Qin there were widespread insurrections that eventually toppled the dynasty. The Han dynasty was established by the warrior party that emerged victorious in the subsequent power struggle. The Han dynasty lasted for nearly four hundred years, with one short interruption in the early years of the Common Era. The Han order left a profound mark on Chinese cultural consciousness, and the Chinese people call themselves and their language Han. The Taoist classic *Masters of Huainan*, heir to the political philosophy of *The Art of War*, dates from the first century of the Han dynasty.

The Era of the Three Kingdoms (190–265 C.E.)

The era of the Three Kingdoms refers to the extended struggle for dominion over the territories of the late Han. China was divided into three competing kingdoms—Wei, Shu, and Wu—vying to reconstruct the decayed empire under their own regimes. Many famous war tales and anecdotes on strategy are taken from this era, which was the time of Zhuge Liang and the notorious general Cao Cao. Cao Cao's own commentaries on *The Art of War* are included in my translation of that classic.

The Jin Dynasty (265–420 C.E.)

The Jin dynasty supplanted Wei, which had emerged victorious among the Three Kingdoms. The Jin dynasty was seriously challenged, and its imperial domains reduced, by other North and Central Asian peoples who set up numerous states collectively known as the Sixteen Kingdoms.

The Northern and Southern Dynasties (420–589 C.E.)

The Northern dynasties were under non-Chinese rule, the Southern dynasties under Chinese rule. During this period there were conflicts both within and between the Northern and Southern dynasties. This period lasted for the better part of the fifth and sixth centuries.

The Sui Dynasty (558–618 C.E.)

The Sui dynasty reunified China in the late sixth century, then collapsed under the duress of rebellions against the government for the exorbitant costs of the policies and programs of the second emperor.

The Tang Dynasty (618–905 C.E.)

Supplanting the Sui, the Tang dynasty lasted for nearly three hundred years and is considered a peak in the cultural history of China. The Chinese empire expanded under the Tang and influenced the development of new nations in Japan, Korea, and Tibet. Buddhism flourished with increased input from India and Central Asia, which then diffused from China into the newer nations surrounding it. China also renewed contact with the West during the Tang dynasty through the entry of Christianity and Islam. As a global power China declined after the peak of the Tang dynasty, reentering centuries of conflicts with other Asian peoples. The tales of war recited by Liu Ji end at the Tang dynasty, range from the Spring and Autumn era to the beginning of the Tang.

LESSONS OF WAR

Calculated Battle

Liu Ji said:

The reasonable course of action in any use of arms starts with calculation. Before fighting, first assess the relative sagacity of the military leadership, the relative strength of the enemy, the sizes of the armies, the lay of the land, and the adequacy of provisions. If you send troops out only after making these calculations, you will never fail to win.

The rule is "Sizing up opponents to determine victory, assessing dangers and distances, is the proper course of action for military leaders" (Sun Tzu, *The Art of War*, "Terrain").

Liu Bei (161–223) was one of the warrior giants of Three Kingdoms fame. He established the kingdom of Shu, or Shu Han, envisioned as a continuation of the Han dynasty in the western part of the Chinese heartland, the ancient region of Shu.

In the last days of the Han dynasty, Liu Bei went three times to ask Zhuge Liang for advice on strategy. Zhuge Liang was to become one of the most famous strategists in history.

Zhuge Liang told Liu Bei, "Ever since the beginning of the current power struggle for what is left of the Han empire, many mettlesome men have arisen. Countless prefectures and districts have been taken over by such men. If you compare current contenders for national power, one of them—the notorious Cao Cao—was once an unknown with a small force, yet he was able to overcome another warlord with a much larger following. The reason the weaker was able to prevail over the stronger is not simply a matter of celestial timing, but also of human planning. Cao Cao now has a million followers; he controls the emperor and gives orders to the lords—he cannot really be opposed.

"Another warlord, in control of the area east of the river, is already the third generation hegemon there. The territory is rugged and the people are loyal to him; the intelligent and capable serve in his employ. He would be a suitable ally, but he cannot be counted on.

"Here there is ease of communication and transport. It is a land suitable for military operations. If its ruler cannot keep it, this would seem to be a boon to a general. Do you have any interest in it? To the southwest are precipitous natural barriers, beyond which lie vast fertile plains. That land is called the heavenly precinct, and it is where the Han dynasty really began.

"Now the governor of that region is ignorant and weak. To the north is the stronghold of the independent Taoist cult of the Celestial Masters. The people are robust and the land is rich, but they do not know how to take care of it. Men of knowledge and ability want to find an enlightened leader.

"General, you are a descendant of the imperial family, and are known everywhere for integrity and justice. You gather heroic men and eagerly seek the wise. If you occupy this whole region, guard the crags and defiles, establish good relations with the foreign tribes to the west and south, make friends with the warlord east of the river, and work to perfect internal organization, then when there is an upheaval in the total political situation and you mobilize your armies, the common people will surely welcome you with food and drink. If you can really do this, hegemony can be established, and the house of Han can be revived."

Liu Bei agreed, and it turned out as planned.

Fighting Schemes

Liu Ji said:

Whenever opponents begin to scheme, attack accordingly, foiling their plans so that they give up.

The rule is "The superior military artist strikes while schemes are being laid" (Sun Tzu, *The Art of War*, "Planning a Siege").

Around 500 B.C.E., in the Spring and Autumn era, the lord of Jin wanted to attack the state of Qi. He sent an emissary to Qi to observe the government there.

The lord of Qi wined and dined the emissary. The wine

flowed freely, and the emissary asked to drink from the lord's cup. This is a gesture of familiarity, and such a request under such circumstances is an insult.

The lord said, "I offer my cup to my guest."

After the emissary of Jin had drunk from the lord's cup, one of the eminent nobles of the Qi court came forward, removed it, and personally continued to serve wine to the emissary in another cup.

Now the emissary, feigning inebriation, stood up in displeasure and said to the highest cabinet official at the court of Qi, "I desire the music of the duke of Zhou. If you can play it, I will dance it for you."

The duke of Zhou was the founder of the Zhou dynasty, which was beginning to disintegrate in the Spring and Autumn era.

The high official of Qi said, "I have not practiced it."

The emissary of Jin left.

The Lord of Qi said to the noble and the official, "Jin is a big state. Now you have angered the emissary of that great state, who came to observe our government. What shall we do?"

The eminent noble said, "I could see the emissary was not ignorant of etiquette, so I would not go along with him when he tried to shame our state."

The cabinet official said, "The music of the duke of Zhou is the music of the national leader. Only a ruler dances it. That emissary is the servant of another, yet he wanted to dance the music of leaders—that is why I didn't perform."

As for the emissary, he went back and reported to the lord of Jin. He said, "Qi cannot be attacked at this time. I tried to insult their lord, and a court noble knew it; I tried to violate their etiquette, and the highest official perceived it."

Confucius said of the court noble who took the lord's cup from the emissary that he "could stop a thrust from a thousand miles away without leaving the table."

Espionage and Warfare

Liu Ji said:

Whenever you move against anyone, before mobilizing the

army first use spies to see whether the opponents are many or few, empty or full, active or quiet. Then you can be very successful and never fail to win in battle.

The rule is "Spies are useful everywhere" (Sun Tzu, *The Art of War*, "On the Use of Spies").

In the sixth century C.E., during the era of the Northern and Southern dynasties, General Wei of the court of Zhou was the military governor of Jade Wall City. General Wei was known for his exemplary behavior in his official capacity. He was skilled at management and able to win people's hearts. All of the spies he sent into the territory of the Qi court did their utmost for him, and certain people of Qi whom Wei had bribed sent him reports by letter. Therefore the Zhou court knew all about the movements of Qi.

Now the prime minister of Qi was a man of sagacity and courage. General Wei loathed him. One of Wei's officers, who knew quite a bit about divination, said, "Next year there will be slaughter in the east." The kingdom of Qi was to the east of Zhou. Wei had this officer compose a song with a double entendre suggesting that the prime minister of Qi was plotting a coup d'état; then he had his secret agents plant this song in the main city of Qi.

Subsequently there developed a rift between the prime minister of Qi and a certain general. When Wei heard of this, he further exacerbated it. The prime minister was eventually executed.

When the ruler of Zhou heard that the prime minister of Qi was dead, he issued an amnesty for that territory, then mobilized a large army to attack, ultimately destroying the kingdom of Qi.

Elite Fighters

Liu Ji said:

Whenever you do battle with opponents, it is imperative to select brave leaders and crack troops to be your vanguard. One purpose of this is to strengthen your own will; another is to break down the opponent's force.

The rule is "Those who do not sort out the levels of skill

among their own troops are the ones who get beaten" (Sun Tzu, *The Art of War*, "Terrain").

In the year 207, two sons of a major warlord of the Three Kingdoms era fled to the north. There they joined forces with a northern tribal people, the Wuheng, who raided Chinese territory from time to time. Cao Cao set out on an expedition north to stop the tribal incursions, intending to strike down the sons of the Chinese warlord as well.

That autumn, with the roads north made impassable by heavy rains, Cao Cao's troops made their way two hundred miles through the hinterland, tunneling through mountains and filling in ravines. They reached north to the territory of the Turanian Xianbei tribes, then headed for the homeland of the Wuheng.

Before Cao Cao's army had gone much more than a hundred miles, they were discovered by the enemy. The brothers, together with several tribal chieftains, led a large force of mounted fighters against them.

Now Cao Cao's equipment was in transport behind him, and few of his soldiers were wearing armor. Everyone was worried.

Cao Cao climbed high up a mountainside to survey the situation. Seeing that their opponents' battle lines were disorderly, he allowed his soldiers to attack, appointing one of his best commanders to lead the vanguard.

The enemy troops were routed. A number of tribal leaders were killed, and many thousand mounted warriors surrendered to the Han Chinese.

Battling on Good Faith

Liu Ji said:

In any battle with an opponent, when soldiers face almost certain death without regret or fear, it is trust that makes them that way. When the leadership is trustworthy and honest, followers are earnest and free from doubt; so there is certain victory in battle.

The rule is "The trustworthy do not cheat" ("Six Secrets," "On Generalship").

During the Three Kingdoms era, the king of Wei personally directed an expedition against the kingdom of Shu. He sent a huge force of light troops under cover to proceed in stealth toward Shu.

Now Zhuge Liang, minister and general of Shu, had taken up a position in the mountains, guarding the passes with well-equipped troops. He had the troops replaced regularly, keeping a contingent of about one-half to one-third the size of the strike force now advancing from Wei to Shu.

The Wei army arrived and set up battle lines just as the Shu guard was in the process of changing. Zhuge's aides urged him to keep the departing troops there for another month to add their strength to the replacements in face of such a powerful enemy force.

Zhuge said, "My command of the military is based on trust and good faith. To lose trust by trying to gain an advantage is a mistake made by men of old. Those who are due to leave pack their gear quickly, waiting for their time to come, while their wives and children stand in their doorways back home, counting the days. Although we are facing a crisis, it will not do to abandon what is right and just."

Thus General Zhuge Liang urged all those whose tour of duty was done to leave the front and return home.

Now those who were scheduled to leave were all so pleased by this announcement that they asked to be allowed to stay for one more battle. They stirred up their courage, determined to fight to the death, saying to each other, "Even if we die, that is still not enough to repay the kindness of Master Zhuge."

On the day of battle, everyone in Zhuge's army rushed forward with drawn sword, each soldier taking on ten of the enemy. They killed one of the Wei leaders, drove off another, and won a great victory in a single battle. This was because of trust and good faith.

Instruction and Warfare

Liu Ji said:

Whenever you want to raise an army, it is necessary first to instruct it in warfare. When the soldiers are trained in ways of scattering and massing, and are thoroughly familiar with the signals for passivity and action, advance and retreat, then when they meet opponents they respond to direction by signals. Then you can do battle without failing to win.

The rule is "To have uninstructed people go into battle is tantamount to abandoning them" (Confucius, *Analects*).

In the Warring States era, the notorious martialist Wu Qi (d. 381 B.C.E.), general of the warring state of Wei, spoke in these terms: "People always die at what they cannot do and are defeated by what is not advantageous to them. The rule for military operations is to start with instruction and training. One person who learns to fight can teach ten people, ten people who learn to fight can teach a hundred people, a hundred can teach a thousand, a thousand can teach ten thousand, ten thousand can teach enough people for three armies.

"Let them learn all the adaptations: maximizing the distance traveled by opponents while minimizing your own, wearing opponents down while staying rested yourselves, starving opponents out while keeping yourselves well fed, knowing when to form a circle and when to form a square, when to sit and when to rise, when to move and when to stop, when to go right and when to go left, when to go ahead and when to fall back, when to split up and when to join, when to band together and when to spread out.

"When they have practiced all of this, then give the fighters weapons. To make them expert in this is called the business of a military leader."

Caring in War

Liu Ji said:

What makes soldiers in battle prefer to charge ahead rather than retreat even for survival is the benevolence of the military leadership. When the soldiers know their leaders care for them as they care for their own children, then the soldiers love their leaders as they do their own fathers. This makes them willing to die in battle, to requite the benevolence of their leaders.

The rule is "Look upon your soldiers as beloved children, and they willingly die with you" (Sun Tzu, *The Art of War*, "Terrain").

During the Warring States era, when the Wei general Wu Qi was military governor of West River, he wore the same clothes and ate the same food as the lowest of his soldiers. He did not use a mat to sit on, and he did not ride when traveling. He personally carried his own bundle of provisions and shared the toil and hardships of the soldiers.

Once, when one of the soldiers was suffering from a festering wound on his arm, the general himself sucked out the pus.

When that soldier's mother heard about this, she began to mourn.

Someone said to her, "Your son is a soldier, yet the general himself sucked the pus from his wound—what is there to mourn about?"

The woman said, "Last year General Wu did the same thing for my husband, and as a result my husband fought in battle without taking a backward step, finally dying at the hands of an enemy. Now that the general has treated my son in this way too, I have no idea where he will die. This is why I mourn him."

It was because Wu Qi was strict with himself while impartial toward others, and had won the hearts of his soldiers, that a Lord of Wei had made him military governor of West River. Wu Qi fought seventy-six major battles with lords of the other warring states, and gained complete victory sixty-four times.

Authority and Warfare

Liu Ji said:

When soldiers in battle forge ahead and do not dare to fall back, this means they fear their own leaders more than they fear the enemy. If they dare to fall back and dare not forge ahead, this means they fear the enemy more than they fear their own leaders. When a general can get his troops to plunge right into the thick of raging combat, it is his authority and sternness that brings this about.

The rule is "To be awesome and yet caring makes a good balance" ("Dialogues of Li, Lord of Wei").

During the Spring and Autumn era, the state of Qi was invaded by the states of Jin and Yan. At first the invaders overcame the military forces of Qi.

One of the eminent nobles of the court of Qi recommended the martialist Tian Rangju to the lord of Qi. To this man, later called Sima Rangju, is attributed the famous military handbook "Sima's Art of War," or "Sima's Rules."

In recommending Rangju, the court noble said to the lord of Qi, "Although Rangju is an illegitimate descendant of a noble family of another state, his culture is attractive to people and his military prowess is awesome to opponents. Please try him."

The lord of Qi then summoned Rangju to discuss military matters with him. The lord was very pleased with what Rangju had to say, and he made him a general, appointing him to lead an army to resist the aggression of the forces of Yan and Jin.

Rangju said, "I am lowly in social status, yet the lord has promoted me from the ranks and placed me above even the grandees. The soldiers are not yet loyal to me, and the common people are not familiar with me; as a man of little account, my authority is slight. I request one of your favorite ministers, someone honored by the state, to be overseer of the army."

The lord acceded to this request and appointed a nobleman to be the overseer. Rangju took his leave, arranging to meet the nobleman at the military headquarters at noon the following day. Then Rangju hastened back to set up a sundial and a waterclock to await the new overseer.

Now this new overseer was a proud and haughty aristocrat, and he imagined that as overseer he was leading his own army. Because of his pride and arrogance, he did not see any need to hurry, in spite of his promise with Rangju the martial master. His relatives and close associates gave him a farewell party, and he stayed to drink with them.

At noon the next day, the new overseer had not arrived at headquarters. Rangju took down the sundial and emptied the waterclock. He assembled the troops and informed them of the agreement with the new overseer.

That evening the nobleman finally arrived. Rangju said to him, "Why are you late?"

He said, "My relatives, who are grandees, gave me a farewell party, so I stayed for that."

Rangju said, "On the day a military leader receives his orders, he forgets about his home; when a promise is made in face of battle, one forgets his family; when the war drums sound, one forgets his own body. Now hostile states have invaded our territory; the state is in an uproar; the soldiers are exposed at the borders; the lord cannot rest easy or enjoy his food; the lives of the common people all depend on you—how can you talk about farewell parties?"

Rangju then summoned the officer in charge of military discipline and asked him, "According to military law, what happens to someone who arrives later than an appointed time?"

The officer replied, "He is supposed to be decapitated."

Terrified, the aristocrat had a messenger rush back to report this to the lord and beseech him for help. But the haughty nobleman was executed before the messenger even returned, and his execution was announced to the army. The soldiers all shook with fear.

Eventually the lord sent an emissary with a letter pardoning the nobleman, who was, after all, the new overseer of the army. The emissary galloped right into camp on horseback with the lord's message.

Rangju said, " 'When a general is in the field, there are orders he doesn't take from the ruler.' "

He also said to the disciplinary officer, "It is a rule that there shall be no galloping through camp, yet now the emissary has done just that. What should be done with him?"

The officer said, "He should be executed."

The emissary was petrified, but Rangju said, "It is not proper to kill an emissary of the lord," and had two of the emissary's attendants executed in his stead. This too was announced to the army.

Rangju sent the emissary back to report to the lord, and then he set out with the army. When the soldiers made camp, Rangju personally oversaw the digging of wells, construction of stoves, preparation of food and drink, and care of the sick. He shared all of the supplies of the leadership with the soldiers, personally eating the same rations as they. He was especially kind to the weary and weakened.

After three days, Rangju called the troops to order. Even those who were ill wanted to go along, eager to go into battle for Rangju. When the armies of Jin and Yan heard about this, they withdrew from the state of Qi. Now Rangju led his troops to chase them down and strike them. Eventually he recovered lost territory and returned with the army victorious.

Reward and Battle

Liu Ji said:

For soldiers to strive to scale high walls in spite of deep moats and showers of arrows and rocks, or for soldiers to plunge eagerly into the fray of battle, they must be induced by serious rewards; then they will prevail over any enemy.

The rule is "Where there are serious rewards, there will be valiant men" ("Three Strategies," also in "Six Secrets").

At the end of the Han dynasty, whenever Cao Cao plundered a city and obtained rare and beautiful objects, he would always use them to reward achievement. To people who had worked hard and were worthy of reward, he would not begrudge even a thousand pieces of gold, while to those without merit he would give nothing. Therefore he was able to win battle after battle.

Punishment and Battle

Liu Ji said:

What will make soldiers in battle dare to go forward and not dare to retreat is a strict penalty for anyone who retreats even an inch. Thus it is possible to gain victory by this means.

The rule is "Punishment should be immediate" ("Sima's Rules," "Duties of the Emperor").

Yang Su (d. 606) was a great general of the brief but momentous Sui dynasty (589–617). His command was strict and orderly; anyone who violated military orders was immediately executed, with no exceptions.

Whenever General Yang was about to face an opponent, he

would look for people to make mistakes so he could execute them. Sometimes over a hundred men would be killed; it was never less than several dozen. He himself would talk and laugh casually as the flowing blood flooded the ground before him.

Then when he faced the enemy on the battle line, he would first command three hundred men to attack. If they were able to break the opponent's battle line, they were all right; if they returned without being able to strike through enemy lines, they would all be executed, regardless of their number.

Then General Yang would send ahead another two or three hundred men, and again killed any who returned. As a result, the commanders and soldiers trembled in fear and were determined to fight to the death. Therefore they consistently won in battle.

Defensive Battle

Liu Ji said:

In any battle, if another is the aggressor and you are the defender, you should not be too quick to fight. If your army is at rest and the soldiers are watching over their homes, you should gather people to guard the cities and fortify the mountain passes, cutting off the aggressors' supply routes. When they do not succeed in drawing you into battle, and their supplies do not reach them, wait until they are worn out and then strike them. If you do this you will always win.

The rule is "Fighting on your own territory is called a ground of dissolution" (Sun Tzu, *The Art of War*, "Nine Grounds").

Wu Di (371–409) was the Martial Emperor of the Later Wei dynasty, a foreign regime in northern China under the rule of the Toba people. He personally led an expedition against the Later Yan dynasty, another foreign regime in northern China, this one under the rule of the Xianbei people, who had invaded Toba territory.

The Wei army failed in its action against Yan, and the Yan emperor wanted to strike back. A military aide came forth, however, and said, "The ancients would first be sure of victory in the planning before going on the offensive. Now there are four reasons why Wei cannot be attacked, and three reasons why Yan should not act."

The emperor of Yan said, "What are these reasons?"

The aide said, "The Wei army is deep inside our territory, and its advantage lies in battle on the open fields; this is one reason why it cannot be attacked. Indeed, it has penetrated so far that it is near our capital, so it is on deadly ground, where the invading soldiers know they have no choice but fight to the death; this is the second reason they cannot be attacked. Furthermore, the vanguard has already been defeated, so the rear lines must have been tightened up; this is the third reason not to attack. Finally, they are many while we are few; this is the fourth reason they cannot be attacked.

"As for the reasons why Yan should refrain from action: first of all, a government army is fighting on its own territory; so we should not act. Second, if it acts and does not prevail, it will be hard to make the hearts of the people resolute; so we should not act. Third, our defenses are not yet ready, and we are not prepared for the coming of an enemy; again, we should not act. These situations are all avoided by warriors.

"It would be best to secure our defenses and wait in ease for the enemy to tire. They have to transport grain over hundreds of miles, and there is nothing in the open fields to take. Eventually they will wear down, so that if they attack, many of their soldiers will die. When their army grows stale and discords develop, then rise up against them and you can overcome them."

The Yan emperor praised the strategic thinking of the military aide.

Offensive Battle

Liu Ji said:

In battle, if the adversary is the defender and you are the invader, just try to penetrate deeply. If you penetrate deeply into their territory, defenders cannot win. This is because of what is called the invader being on heavy ground while the defender is on light ground.

The rule is "Invaders become more intense the further

they enter alien territory" (Sun Tzu, *The Art of War*, "Nine Grounds").

In the early Han dynasty, Han Xin (d. 196 B.C.E.) and Zhang Er (d. 202 B.C.E.) mobilized an army of several tens of thousands to attack the state of Zhao. Han Xin was an outstanding militarist involved in the wars waged to establish the Han dynasty. Zhang Er was one of a number of local feudal kings whose states were allowed to exist within the structure of the early Han empire.

Now the king of Zhao and the lord of Cheng-an massed an army of two hundred thousand men at a strategic pass, to defend against the invaders. One of the councillors of Zhao, however, said to the lord of Cheng-an, "I hear that Han Xin's army has been campaigning successfully, and now, reinforced by Zhang Er's army, he wants to descend on Zhao. His string of victories has taken him from his own land to fight far abroad; news of his power robs people of their courage, and it is impossible to stand up to him directly.

"I hear that Han Xin is transporting supplies from a great distance. The soldiers have the look of hunger; they eat irregularly and never sleep on full stomachs. Now the road through the pass is too narrow for two cars to travel abreast, or for a group of horsemen to ride in formation; so their supplies must be behind them.

"Please let me take a special force of thirty thousand to cut their supply lines off from the byways. You secure your fortifications and don't fight with them. They cannot go forward; they cannot return; they cannot plunder anything from the field. Before ten days are up, the heads of both leaders, Han Xin and Zhang Er, can be hanging from your flagpole. Please pay heed; otherwise you will be captured."

But the lord of Cheng-an was self-righteous and did not listen to this strategy. Eventually he was killed.

Strength and Battle

Liu Ji said:

Whenever you fight with opponents, if you are numerous and strong, you can feign weakness to entice opponents who will think little of coming to fight with you. Strike them with your best soldiers, and their forces will be defeated.

The rule is "Though effective, appear to be ineffective" (Sun Tzu, *The Art of War*, "Strategic Assessments").

Late in the era of the Warring States, a general of the state of Zhao named Li Mu (d. 228 B.C.E.) was permanently stationed on the northwest frontier to defend Chinese territory against incursions by the Huns. For convenience, he set up an office to collect taxes and forward them to his headquarters at the front, where he spent them on the soldiers. Every day he had cattle slaughtered to feed the troops well.

General Li had the soldiers practice mounted archery and watch over their signal fires, and he employed many spies and informants. Afterwards he made his commanders and soldiers promise to pull back into a closed defense and not to fight whenever the Huns came. Anyone who dared to take a Hun captive was to be executed.

They did this for several years, and although nothing was lost to the Huns, they considered Li Mu a coward. Even the Zhao frontier troops thought their leader was timid. The king of Zhao remonstrated with General Li, but the general continued to do as before.

Finally, the king recalled General Li and replaced him with someone else. Now, under their new leader, the Chinese garrison soldiers went out and fought whenever the Huns showed up. After little more than a year the Chinese had taken several beatings from the Huns and had suffered considerable loss. As a result, it was impossible to farm or raise animals in the frontier region.

Now Li Mu was asked to take over once again, but he claimed to be ill and refused to leave home. The king pressed him to lead the army, so Li finally agreed on the condition that he be allowed to pursue his former policy. The king accepted this provision, so General Li went back and followed his original plan. The Huns came again, but though they didn't get anything, they thought General Li was a weakling.

The frontier soldiers won prizes every day, but prizes were not what they wanted. What all of them wanted was a fight. Now

General Li had thirteen hundred specially selected chariots outfitted and picked out thirteen thousand horsemen, fifty thousand seasoned soldiers, and a hundred thousand archers. All of them drilled and practiced combat.

Now the military authorities allowed the local people to let their flocks and herds out. People filled the fields. When the Huns showed up, General Li pretended to be at a loss and even let them take several thousand captives.

When the Hun chieftain heard about this, he led a huge crowd on a mass raid into Chinese territory.

General Li set up many surprise battle lines and had his army fan out on both sides to attack. In this way the Chinese routed the Huns. They killed over a hundred thousand horsemen and put the tribal chieftain to flight.

For more than ten years after that the Huns did not dare to cross the border of Zhao.

Weakness and Battle

Liu Ji said:

Whenever you do battle with opponents who outnumber you and are stronger than you, you should set up many banners and increase the number of stoves you build, giving the appearance of strength to prevent opponents from figuring out your numbers and power. Then adversaries will not be quick to fight with you. If you can leave quickly, then your whole army can escape harm.

The rule is "Strength and weakness are a matter of formation" (Sun Tzu, *The Art of War*, "Force").

During the Later Han dynasty (25–219), a group of the semi-nomadic Qiang people of Central Asia, who were ancestors of the modern Tibetans, revolted against the Han Chinese empire. The Han empress dowager appointed a leading strategist to be the military governor of that area, but a horde of several thousand Qiang cut off the new governor's march.

The governor stopped his troops immediately and announced that he was going to send to the imperial court for reinforcements. Learning of this, the Qiang divided up to comb the surrounding countryside, looking for the Chinese messengers who had been sent to the Han court for help.

Now that the Qiang militia was scattered, the Chinese governor proceeded by forced marches night and day, covering over thirty miles a day. He had each mess sergeant make two stoves at first, and then increase the number of stoves each day. The Qiang did not dare to attack.

Someone said to the governor, "The famous martialist Sun Bin decreased his campfires, while you increased them. Also, you went more than three times the maximum daily march recommended in military classics. Why is this?"

The governor said, "The enemy had many soldiers, I had few. I increased the fire stoves to make them think the local militia was coming to welcome us. Thinking we are many and traveling fast, they hesitate to pursue us. Sun Bin saw weakness; I give the appearance of strength. The situations are not the same."

Hauteur and Battle

Liu Ji said:

When your opponents are strong and outnumber you, so that you cannot be sure of prevailing, you should use humility and courtesy to make them haughty, then wait for an opening that offers an opportunity of which you can take advantage, and you can beat them.

The rule is "Use humility to make them haughty" (Sun Tzu, *The Art of War*, "Strategic Assessments").

During the era of the Three Kingdoms, warlords of Wei in the north, Wu in the south, and Shu in the west struggled among one another for hegemony over the remains of the Chinese empire. At one point a leading general of Shu made a foray north, where he captured one Wei general and surrounded another.

Now the general of Wu who was stationed at the border with Wei and Shu left his post on account of illness. He was visited by another Wu general, who said to him. "The Shu general is right on the border—why did you leave? There will be trouble if no one stands in his way."

The retired Wu general said, "You are right, but I am very ill."

The other Wu general said, "The Shu general is proud of his achievements, and his hauteur is overbearing. He has also heard of your illness, and is surely that more the lax in his precautions. If you attack now, when he isn't expecting it, you can capture or restrain him. This would be a good strategy to present to the king."

The retired Wu general said, "The Shu general is a brave and mettlesome man. He is already hard to oppose on this account. Furthermore, he has taken control of strategic territory, where he has won great prestige. With his recent successes and his growing boldness, it is not easy to plot against him."

When the retired Wu general got to the capital city, the king of Wu asked him, "If you are ill, who can replace you?"

The retired general recommended the other Wu general, with whom he had had the foregoing conversation, saying, "He is a deep thinker and has the ability to bear responsibility. Considering his orderly thinking, I regard him as suitable for this important post. Furthermore, he is not yet well known, so the general of Shu doesn't hate him. No one could be better. If you give him the job, have him conceal his actions outwardly while inwardly looking for opportunities to take advantage; then he can overcome the general of Shu."

So the king of Wu summoned the other general and promoted him. When this new Wu general of the border guard arrived at the frontier region, he sent a letter to the Shu general. The letter was fawning and obsequious, flattering the Shu general. The Wu general also wrote to the Shu general of his concern about the leading warlord of Wei and expressed hope that the general of Shu would contain this menace.

When the Shu general read this letter, he noted the humility expressed by the general of Wu and his desire for the good will of Shu. As a result, the general of Shu relaxed and was no longer hostile. Now the general of Wu reported this to the king of Wu, and explained how the Shu general could be captured.

So the king of Wu sent an undercover force up north, appointing two generals to lead the vanguard. In this way, the kingdom of Wu was able to wrest important territory from the grip of the warrior general of Shu.

Diplomatic Relations

Liu Ji said:

Whenever you go to war, establish cordial relations with neighboring countries. Form alliances to draw them into helping you. If you attack your enemies from the front while your allies attack from behind, your enemies will surely be vanquished.

The rule is "On intersecting ground, form communications" (Sun Tzu, *The Art of War*, "Nine Grounds").

During the era of the Three Kingdoms, at one point the top general of Shu had one of the Wei generals surrounded. The high command of Wei sent another general to the rescue. As it happened, the waters of the Han River rose violently, enabling the Shu general to capture the leader of the Wei reinforcements, with a large contingent of infantry and cavalry. The Shu general sent his own troops shooting down the swollen river in boats to strike the Wei forces.

Now at this time the puppet emperor of the dissolving Han dynasty had his temporary capital not far from the war zone. Cao Cao, the Wei warlord general who manipulated the puppet emperor, thought the capital was too close to enemy lines, and he wanted to move it out of reach.

One of the great ministers of Wei, however, objected to Cao Cao's plan. He said, "The reinforcements we sent were overcome by the river—it is not that they failed in defensive battle. As far as the overall policy of the state is concerned, nothing is lost; so if we move the capital now, this will come across to the enemy as a sign of weakness, and it will also make the local populace uneasy.

"The king of Wu and the king of Shu are outwardly close but inwardly distant; now that the top general of Shu is getting his way, the king of Wu is no doubt displeased. We should induce the king of Wu to stop the Shu general from behind— then the siege surrounding our Wei general will automatically be lifted."

Cao Cao followed this suggestion and sent an emissary to

establish an alliance with the king of Wu. Subsequently the king of Wu sent one of his generals to attack the territory of the Shu warlord general, and the Wu general was able to wrest two districts from the grip of Shu. As a result, the general of Shu finally abandoned his siege of the Wei army and left the region.

Formation and Battle

Liu Ji said:

Whenever you do battle, if the enemy army is very large, then set up false formations as feints to divert and divide the enemy forces by inducing them to believe they have to divide their troops to defend against you. Once the enemy forces are divided, there will be relatively few troops in each contingent. You can concentrate your forces into one, so as to outnumber each group of enemy soldiers. Strike few with many, and you will not fail to win.

The rule is "Induce others to construct a formation while you yourself are formless" (Sun Tzu, *The Art of War*, "Emptiness and Fullness").

In the year 200, near the end of the moribund Han dynasty, the warlord Cao Cao faced off with one of his main competitors. His opponent sent two strategists with a top commander to lead an attack on an army led by one of Cao Cao's men, while he himself led another force to follow up.

As for Cao Cao, he went to rescue his men, who were now under siege. One of his advisors, however, warned him that he had too few troops with him to do battle, and that it would be necessary to divide the enemy's forces. Consequently, following the plan outlined by his advisor, Cao Cao led a contingent up behind his adversary, who thus had to send part of his own force back to deal with Cao Cao.

Now Cao Cao led his army on a forced march toward the position being held by his other troops under siege. When they were nearly there, the opposing commander took fright and turned around to fight Cao Cao's newly arrived reinforcements.

Now that the opponents' forces were divided, Cao Cao had two top generals launch a devastating attack, killing the enemy commander and lifting the siege.

Momentum and Battle

Liu Ji said:

In battle, momentum means riding on the force of the tide of events. If enemies are on the way to destruction, then you follow up and press them; their armies will surely collapse.

The rule is "Use the force of momentum to defeat them" ("Three Strategies").

In 265, the Martial Emperor of Jin founded the Jin dynasty, heralding the end of the era of the Three Kingdoms. Establishing himself by overthrowing the dynasty set up by Cao Cao in the northern kingdom of Wei, the Martial Emperor of Jin also had a secret plan to destroy the southern kingdom of Wu. Many of his courtiers, however, were opposed to the idea of attacking Wu.

Only three of the Martial Emperor's ministers were in favor of his plan to destroy Wu. One of them was ultimately appointed military director of the border region.

When the new military director of the border region reached his command outpost, he had the soldiers' armor and equipment repaired, and polished up their martial skills. Finally he selected a special force of elite troops, who then launched a successful assault against the army of one of the leading generals of Wu.

Now the military director petitioned the Jin emperor for permission to make a full-scale attack on the kingdom of Wu. The emperor sent back a message telling the director to wait until the following year for such a massive undertaking.

But the military director wrote a letter back to the emperor, explaining the situation in these terms:

"In any affair, it is imperative to compare gain and loss. With this invasion, the prospects of gain are 80 to 90 percent, while the prospects of loss are 10 to 20 percent. If we stop, nothing will be accomplished. The courtiers say we can be beat, but they cannot tell. It is just that they are not the strategists, so they get no credit for our military successes. They are all embarrassed at having spoken in error before, so they oppose this undertaking.

"Since autumn our movements against the enemy have become obvious; if we stop now, they might develop a scheme in fear—they may move the capital, increase fortifications, and relocate the populace. If their citadels cannot be attacked and there is no plunder in the countryside, next year may be too late to carry out our plans."

When this letter from the military director of the border region arrived at the capital, the emperor happened to be playing chess with one of the ministers who did approve of the emperor's plan to destroy the kingdom of Wu. The minister said, "Your Majesty is highly intelligent and has great military acumen. Your nation is rich and your armies are strong. The king of Wu is decadent and vicious, killing off the worthy and able. If you attack him now, the matter can be settled without much effort."

The emperor then gave his permission to move against the kingdom of Wu. Now the military director of the border region launched his campaign, scoring successive military victories and winning over the provinces of Wu as the provincial authorities defected from Wu and switched their allegiance to Jin.

That summer there was heavy flooding, and the commanders of the Jin army suggested to the military director that they wait until winter to go on the move again, as floods always brought epidemics. The director, however, said that a long entrenched enemy cannot easily be overcome, and insisted on riding the momentum of their victories all the way to the final overthrow of the king of Wu.

Pursuing this course of action, the Jin army encountered little further resistance. Finally, in the year 280, the Jin dynasty annexed the former kingdom of Wu.

Knowledge and Battle

Liu Ji said:

Whenever you mobilize an army to attack an enemy, it is imperative to know the location of battle. When your army gets there, if you can induce the enemy forces to come when you expect them, you will win in battle. If you know the place and time of battle, then your preparations will be concentrated and your defenses will be firm.

The rule is "When you know the place and time of battle, then you can join the fight from a thousand miles away" (Sun Tzu, *The Art of War*, "Emptiness and Fullness").

During the Warring States era, the states of Wei and Zhao attacked the state of Han, which appealed to the state of Qi for help in this emergency.

The government of Qi sent one of its generals with an army, which marched directly for the capital of Wei, the aggressor. When the invading Wei general heard of this, he left the state of Han and returned to Wei.

Now the Qi general received some advice from Sun Bin, a noted strategist and descendant of the famous Sun Wu (Sun Tzu), legendary author of *The Art of War*. Master Sun said, "The armies of Wei, Zhao, and Han are fierce and think little of Qi, which they regard as cowardly. A good warrior would take advantage of this tendency and 'lead them on with prospects of gain.'

"According to *The Art of War*, struggling for an advantage fifty miles away will thwart the forward leadership, and only half of those who chase prospects of gain twenty-five miles away will actually get there. Have the army of Qi enter Wei territory and make thousands of campfires; on the next day have them make half that number of campfires, and on the next day have them make half again that number."

The Qi army did as Sun Bin had advised. The Wei general was delighted to hear that the number of campfires was dwindling day by day, thinking that the men of Qi were defecting. He said, "I knew the soldiers of Qi were cowards—they've been in our territory for only three days now, and more than half the army has run away."

Consequently, the Wei general left his infantry behind and hastened in pursuit of the Qi army with only a personal force of crack troops. Calculating the speed of their pursuit, Sun Bin concluded that by nightfall the Wei force would reach an area of narrow roads and difficult passage, a place suitable for ambush.

Now Sun Bin had a large tree cut down and stripped of its bark. On the bare log he wrote, "The general of Wei will die at this tree," and had it placed on the road where the Wei troops would pass that night. Then he had several thousand expert archers conceal themselves near the road.

When the Wei general came to the place where the stripped log had been set across the road, he lit a torch to read what had been written on it. Before he finished reading, the archers of Qi, for whom the kindling of the torch became a signal to fire, loosed their arrows all at once, throwing the Wei troops into a panic. Realizing he had been outwitted and his men were beaten, the Wei general killed himself.

Reconnaissance

Liu Ji said:

The first rule of maneuvering an army is to send out scouts for reconnaissance. Small brigades of scouts, keeping a fixed distance from the moving army, reconnoiter in all directions. If they see a hostile army, they relay this information back to the commander, who then directs the soldiers to prepare.

The rule is "Those who face the unprepared with preparation are victorious" (Sun Tzu, *The Art of War*, "Planning a Seige").

In the first century B.C.E., during the Han dynasty, one of the tribes of the ancient Qiang people rebelled against the Chinese empire. They broke into frontier fortifications, attacked cities, and killed officials.

At that time a certain Rear General Zhao (137–52 B.C.E.) was over seventy years old; the emperor considered him too old for warfare, and sent a messenger to ask the general to nominate a replacement.

The general said, "Hearing about something a hundred times is not as good as seeing it once. It is hard to predict the course of a military operation, so let me ride out to see conditions for myself so that I can present a plan."

He added, "The Qiang rebels are a small minority tribe and cannot last long in defiance of a major power. Please leave this up to me, old as I am, and don't worry about it."

The emperor smiled and gave him permission.

When the Chinese general reached the disturbed area, he

commandeered a cavalry of ten thousand mounted warriors. To move against the Qiang they had to cross a river, but the general feared that the Qiang might cut them off, so he first sent three groups to cross by night. When they reached the other side, they set up a battle line, and the rest of the cavalry crossed over the next morning.

Hundreds of Qiang riders appeared, watching the Chinese cavalry from the side. The Chinese general said to his troops, "Our warriors and horses have just arrived and are tired out, so do not give chase to the Qiang. They are all expert horsemen, difficult to stop, and our soldiers might be tempted to pursue them. Our aim in striking this rebellious tribe is to exterminate them, so let us not be eager for small gains."

Thus commanding his men not to attack the Qiang, the general sent riders out to reconnoiter the mountain ahead. The scouts did not find any of the Qiang tribesmen, and the cavalry crossed the mountain in the middle of the night.

The general called his officers together for a conference and said, "I know the Qiang rebels cannot do anything. If they had sent several thousand men to guard the mountain, how could our troops have penetrated this far?"

So the general saw to it that there was constant reconnaissance, sending scouts out to considerable distances. Whenever he moved his troops he made preparations for battle, and when they stopped they built fortified camps. The old general was well able to bear this heavy responsibility, and he looked after his warriors very well. He never fought without strategic planning and eventually succeeded in pacifying the region.

Striving in Battle

Liu Ji said:

Whenever you engage in warfare with enemies, you should strive to be the first to occupy advantageous terrain, so that you can win in battle. If the enemy gets there first, do not attack; wait for a change such that you can strike advantageously.

The rule is "Let there be no attack on a ground of contention" (Sun Tzu, *The Art of War*, "Nine Grounds").

In the year 234, during the era of the Three Kingdoms, the kingdom of Shu sent an army out on the road north, toward the kingdom of Wei. One of the military leaders of Wei warned his people that the Shu army was intending to occupy the northern plain, but there were those who disagreed.

One of the great generals of Wei, however, thought that this advisor was correct, and he stationed a garrison in the northern plain before the Shu forces arrived. The Wei garrison had not yet finished building fortifications when a huge army from Shu showed up.

The Wei forces struck back, and after a few days the Shu general led his army west. Most of the Wei commanders thought the Shu army was going to attack the western provinces of Wei; one of them, however, disagreed, saying that the Shu general was just making things look that way as a strategic ruse to lure the Wei forces west, whereas the real intention of the Shu general was to attack the east.

That night the Shu army did in fact attack in the east. Because of the warning of the perceptive commander, however, the Wei army was prepared and did not suffer a loss.

Going on the Attack

Liu Ji said:

In warfare, attack is a matter of knowing the adversary. If you send out troops only when you know that the adversary is vulnerable for some reason and can be defeated, then you will not fail to win.

The rule is "Vulnerability is a matter of attack" (Sun Tzu, *The Art of War*, "Formation").

During the era of the Three Kingdoms, the warlord general Cao Cao of Wei sent one of his generals to be the military governor of a border area. This Wei general garrisoned his troops there, making many rice fields. He also sent secret agents into the kingdom of Wu to the south, to invite the cooperation of a group of dissidents within that kingdom.

One of the leading generals of Wu said, "The land where the Wei army is garrisoned is very fertile. Once they harvest a crop of rice there, their numbers will surely increase. If this goes on for a few years, Cao Cao will be hard to stop. We should get rid of them as soon as possible."

So the Wu general made a report on these conditions to the king of Wu, who then personally went on the expedition against Cao Cao's garrison. The Wu forces got there in a day and a night. The king asked his generals about strategy, and they all suggested making a high fortification, which they said could with effort be built rapidly.

But the leading Wu general said, "They have already fortified the city they occupy, and reinforcements are sure to be arriving, making it impossible to get at them. Now the rains are starting, and we should take this opportunity to attack; for if we stay a few days we will surely return exhausted, and the roads back will be difficult. I think that would be dangerous.

"Now as I see this city, it is not all that secure. If we attack it on four sides while our armed forces are at their keenest, the Wei occupation army can be thrown out in a short time, and we can get back home before the rivers swell. This is the way to complete victory."

The king of Wu followed this advice. The Wu forces staged an all-out attack on the city and very soon overthrew the Wei occupation. The leader of the Wei reinforcements was on the road when he heard the news that the city had fallen, and he promptly withdrew on learning of Wei's defeat.

As for the Wu general who had recommended this successful course of action, the king of Wu rewarded him for his achievement, making him military governor of the area.

Defense and Battle

Liu Ji said:

In warfare, the defender is the one who knows himself. If you know you have no reasonable chance of winning, then for the time being stay firmly on the defensive, waiting for a time when the adversary can be beaten. If you wait for the right time to attack, you will always win.

The rule is "Invincibility is a matter of defense" (Sun Tzu, *The Art of War*, "Formation").

Around the middle of the second century B.C.E., during the reign of the fourth-generation emperor of the Han dynasty, seven states—Wu, Chu, and five others—rebelled against imperial authority and tried to secede from the empire. The emperor appointed one of his distinguished generals to lead the reprisals against the rebellious eastern states.

The general made a petition to the emperor, stating, "The armed forces of Chu are highly mobile and hard to fight. Let us cede the state of Liang to them and then cut off their supply routes. If we do this, we can stop them."

The emperor agreed to this, and the general went out to join the army.

Right at that time, the Wu army was attacking the state of Liang, and the local government of Liang, in desperation, asked the imperial Han general for help.

But the general led his troops northeast to a walled city and took up a defensive position there. The king of Liang sent an emissary to plead with the imperial general, but the general kept to his ploy and did not go to the rescue.

Now the king of Liang sent an appeal to the emperor himself. The emperor ordered his general to rescue Liang, but the general did not obey the command; instead he fortified the city walls and refused to come out. In the meanwhile, he sent mounted commanders out to cut off the supply routes behind the armies of Wu and Chu.

When the armies of Wu and Chu ran low on supplies and were getting so hungry they wanted to go home, they tried to provoke the imperial general into a fight several times. The general, however, never came out.

One night there was a fearful commotion in the camp of the imperial general, as fighting started. The fighting spread to the skirts of the general's tent, but he lay there stoically and would not get up. After a while the disturbance died down.

The Wu army rushed the southeast corner of the city, so the imperial general had defenses built up on the northwest perimeter. Before long the Wu army did in fact rush the northwest wall, but they could not get in.

Now the armies of Wu and Chu were starving, so they withdrew and started back to their homelands. At this point the imperial general sent his best soldiers out to run them down, and his men routed the troops of Wu and Chu.

The king of Chu abandoned his armed forces and ran away

with a few thousand bodyguards to hole up south of the Long River. The army of the Han empire now took advantage of this victory to chase the Chu armies down and catch them all, conquering the territories of Chu.

The imperial general of the Han sent out an order, saying, "Anyone who gets the king of Wu will be given a reward of a thousand pieces of gold."

In little more than a month, a man of Yue, a state neighboring Wu, showed up with the head of the king of Wu.

The whole civil war had taken seven months; Wu and Chu were completely pacified.

Postponing Battle

Liu Ji said:

In war, when adversaries are orderly in their movements and are at their sharpest, it is not yet time to fight with them; it is best to fortify your position and wait. Watch for their energy to wane after being on alert for a long time; then rise and strike them. You will not fail to win.

The rule is "Delay until others wane" ("Zuo Family Tradition on the Spring and Autumn Annals").

In the early days of the Tang dynasty (618–905), the founder of the dynasty campaigned against a warlord who had taken over territorial rule at the end of the preceding Sui dynasty (588–618). When the Tang founder surrounded the warlord in the ancient eastern capital, the leader of a concurrent peasant rebellion brought his whole following to rescue the Sui warlord. The Tang founder, however, blocked the peasant army at an outlying mountain pass called "Military Fastness."

When the peasant army massed east of the river, stretching over miles, all the commanders in the Tang founder's army looked frightened. The founder himself rode high up the mountain with a few horsemen to view the peasant army.

Seeing the masses, the founder of the Tang dynasty said, "This mob has never seen a major adversary, and now it is going through a narrow defile in a chaotic condition, without order in the army. The fact that they are massing near the city means they think lightly of us. I think that if our forces do not move, but wait for their spirits to wind down, after they have been in the field for a long time the fighters will get hungry and will surely withdraw on their own. If we then strike them as they are pulling out, we can surely overcome them."

The peasant army stayed in battle formation from before dawn until after noon. The fighters got hungry and tired, and began looking around and fighting over food and drink.

Now the Tang founder had one of his commanders lead three hundred mounted warriors south to gallop past the western flank of the mob, giving these instructions: "If the mob doesn't stir when you charge past, stop and come back. If you sense them stirring, turn and charge east."

When the horsemen galloped past, the peasants did stir, and the Tang founder gave the word to attack. They charged down from the mountainside into the valley, following the valley east and attacking the insurgents from behind.

The leader of the peasants, once a military officer, led his fighters away, but before they could regroup, the Tang founder struck them with light mounted troops, mowing them down wherever they went. The mob scattered to the four winds, and their leader was captured alive, only to be killed later in the capital city of the new Tang empire, in the year 621.

Emptiness in Battle

Liu Ji said:

In warfare, if you are void of power, you feign the appearance of fullness in such a way the enemies cannot tell how empty or powerful you really are. Then they will be hesitant to engage you in battle, and you can keep your forces intact.

The rule is "When opponents are unwilling to fight with you, it is because they think it is contrary to their interests, or because you have misled them into thinking so" (Sun Tzu, *The Art of War*, "Emptiness and Fullness," Liu Ji's own paraphrase).

During the era of the Three Kingdoms, when Zhuge Liang, general of the kingdom of Shu, was stationed at one of the most critical strategic passes on the border of the kingdom of Wei, he was left alone to guard the fortress with ten thousand troops when the other Shu generals went south with their armies.

Now Sima Yi, general of the kingdom of Wei, led twenty thousand troops to attack Zhuge Liang. When they reached a point some twenty miles from the Shu outpost, Sima Yi sent scouts to reconnoiter. When the scouts returned, they reported that Zhuge Liang had little manpower in the citadel.

Meanwhile, Zhuge Liang also knew of the imminent arrival of the Wei army; he feared he might be hard pressed and wanted to recall one of the other Shu generals, who had left earlier with his troops. They were already too far away, however, and there was nothing they could do to help.

Now the defending Shu commanders and officers paled in fear, for none of them knew what to do. Zhuge Liang, however, remained composed. He ordered his soldiers to take down the banners, put away the war drums, and stay inside as much as possible. He also had all the gates of the walled city opened and the streets cleaned.

Sima Yi, the Wei general, had thought that Zhuge Liang was being cautious; and now that he saw this apparent weakness, he suspected that there were ambushers lying in wait. So he led his troops back up into the mountains to the north.

The next day at mealtime, Zhuge Liang was laughing with his assistants, saying, "No doubt Sima Yi thought I was only feigning weakness and must have had ambushers hidden, so he ran off through the mountains!"

Battling with the Full

Liu Ji said:

In warfare, if your opponents are full of power, be well prepared and they will not readily make any moves.

The rule is "When they are fulfilled, be prepared against them" (Sun Tzu, *The Art of War*, "Strategic Assessments").

In the early days of the era of the Three Kingdoms, when the first ruler of the kingdom of Shu originally established himself as a local king of a part of the region of Shu, he appointed a formidable warrior as forward general, handing him a ceremonial axe of authority. The same year the forward general garrisoned an army on the border of the kingdom of Wu; he also led a siege against the army of one of the generals of the kingdom of Wei.

Cao Cao, one of the leading warriors of Wei, sent a commander with some troops to rescue his brother general, now being besieged by the forward general of Shu. That autumn there were heavy rains, however, causing the Han River to flood, thus drowning the troops sent by Cao Cao. The chief commander of these troops surrendered to the forward general of Shu, and another of the Wei commanders was also captured.

Some dissident factions within the kingdom of Wei also accepted orders from the forward general of Shu and became his supporters. As a result, the power of the warrior of Shu shook all of China.

Fighting Too Readily

Liu Ji said:

Whenever you are going to fight with an enemy, you must measure the adversary carefully before you send out armed forces. If you sally forth recklessly and fight without a plan, you will surely be defeated by the enemy.

The rule is "The bold will readily clash, readily clash without knowing what is to their advantage" (Wu Qi, "On Generalship").

During the Spring and Autumn era, the state of Jin fought a war with the state of Chu. The lord of Jin knew that the Chu general was short tempered and impulsive; so he seized the Chu ambassador to anger the general.

Enraged, the Chu general did in fact attack the Jin army, and his forces were routed.

Using Profit to Fight

Liu Ji said:

Whenever you are at war, if the opponent's general is stupid and inflexible, he can be lured with the prospect of gain. When the opponent is so greedy to get something that he is not mindful of danger, you can overcome him by ambush.

The rule is "Draw them in with the prospect of gain" (Sun Tzu, *The Art of War*, "Strategic Assessments").

During the Spring and Autumn era, the state of Chu attacked the state of Jiao. One of the offiicals of Chu said, "Jiao is small but volatile. Being volatile, it is no doubt lacking in planning. Let us use unarmed men disguised as woodcutters for bait."

This plan was followed, and the Jiao side captured thirty men. The next day men of Jiao came out to fight and chased the men of Chu into the mountains.

Now there were Chu people sitting on the northern perimeter of the citadel of Jiao, and others lying in wait in the mountains; so when the men of Jiao chased the Chu agents into the mountains, they ran into the ambush and suffered a heavy defeat.

Fighting Attackers

Liu Ji said:

When you and your rivals are keeping to your respective borders, if rivals plunder your territory and thus disturb the populace in the outlying areas, you could set up ambushes at natural barriers, or you can construct artificial barriers against them, so that enemies will not readily try to invade.

The rule is "What discourages opponents from coming is the prospect of harm" (Sun Tzu, *The Art of War*, "Emptiness and Fullness").

Around the beginning of the eighth century, when the illustrious Tang dynasty (618–905) was nearly a hundred years old, there was a problem between the Chinese empire and a Turkic people known in Chinese as the Tuque. At one point the general overseer of the north, an officer of the imperial Chinese organization, was beaten in a battle with the Turks. He then summoned a high minister of the Tang court to lead an attack against the Turks.

The marauding Turks had already left the immediate vicinity when the imperial minister arrived. He led his troops after them, and attacked their camp that very night, routing them.

At first the Turks and the North Army of Tang China had recognized the Yellow River as the boundary between their territories. On the north bank there was a place where the Turks would go to pray at their shrine each time they were going to raid Chinese territory to the south.

Now at this time one of the Turkic khans, who was eventually to be khan of all the Turks, made a sudden all-out attack on the western Turks. The Chinese minister-general who had come from court to lead the punitive expedition took advantage of this drain on the Turks to seize territory north of the river to build a defensive fortress. The Chinese called this fortress "Citadel of Accepting Surrender," after the fortress built eight centuries earlier by the Han dynasty Chinese to stop the incursions of the Huns. This was the way the minister-general intended to stop the Turks from raiding Chinese territory to the south.

One of the Tang grandees objected that the line of defense against northern tribes was traditionally set south of the river, and if this citadel were built on the rangeland of the Turks, it would inevitably wind up in their hands. The minister-general, who had, after all, gone at the request of the general overseer of the north, insisted on having the fortress built, and the emperor of China finally gave his permission.

The minister-general proposed to keep the garrison troops there for a year to help with the work. Two hundred men ran away to go home, but the minister-general had them caught and killed at the wall of the fortress. The whole army shook in fear, and the draftees worked as hard as they could. As a result, three fortresses were built in sixty days.

The fortresses were over a hundred miles apart and bordered on the northern desert. The Chinese army opened up a hundred miles of territory and set up a watch post with eighteen hundred troops on a mountain further north.

From then on the Turks did not dare to come over the mountains to graze their horses, and there were no more yearly raids on the northern territories of Tang-dynasty China. Enormous expenditures were thus eliminated, and the garrison army was greatly reduced.

Fearlessness in Danger

Liu Ji said:

When you battle with opponents, if you fall into a situation where there is danger of destruction, you should inspire your soldiers to fight to the death, for they will win if they forget about surviving.

The rule is "When warriors are in great danger, then they have no fear" (Sun Tzu, *The Art of War*, "Nine Grounds").

The monumental Han dynasty of China lasted for more than four hundred years, with but a brief interruption in the middle, about two thousand years ago. During this hiatus after two centuries of the dynasty, a certain military commander set himself up as king of Shu in western China.

Now one of the loyalist generals of the Han dynasty invaded Shu to attack the warlord king. The Han loyalist overthrew a district of Shu, and all the fortresses in the area surrendered.

The emperor of China, however, warned the general, "There are over a hundred thousand troops in the capital of Shu, so it will not do to take them lightly. Just occupy the position you have taken; if they come to attack you, don't fight with them. If they don't come after you, then move your encampments up to pressure them. When they grow weary, then you may attack them."

But the loyalist general didn't listen to the emperor's advice. Taking advantage of the gains he had already made, he personally led a cavalry over two hundred thousand strong to ride against the capital city of Shu.

When he came within a few miles of the walled city, the general set up camp on the north bank of the river. Then he had pontoon bridges made and sent another general to garrison about seven miles away, south of the river.

Now the emperor was alarmed. He upbraided the loyalist general in a letter, saying, "After all my instructions, how can you disobey me? Now you have entered deeply into enemy territory, and you have set up separate camps. Your two camps won't be able to reach each other in an emergency. If the enemy sends a brigade to pin you down and attacks the other camp in force, once the others are defeated you will be beaten. Please take your army back to your stronghold."

But before the imperial message had reached his general, the self-proclaimed king of Shu actually did send a hundred thousand soldiers to attack one camp of Han loyalists, and another hundred thousand soldiers to block the other camp, preventing the two generals of the Han dynasty from helping each other.

The forces of the first loyalist general staged a tremendous battle that lasted all day, but they got the worst of it and ran inside the walls of the city they had occupied. Now the army of the king of Shu surrounded them.

At this point the Han general called his commanders together and tried to rouse their spirits, speaking to them in these terms: "We have crossed the most rugged territory together and have fought our way over hundreds of miles, winning everywhere. Now we have penetrated deeply into enemy territory and are near the capital city. But we and our ally camp are both under siege, and we can't join forces. It is hard to tell what might happen. I want to send an undercover force to join up with our ally camp south of the river. If we can cooperate with like minds, people will fight of their own accord, and much can be accomplished. Otherwise we will suffer a total loss. The chance to win or lose is in this one operation."

The commanders agreed.

So they closed the camp and stayed inside for three days while they feasted the soldiers and fed the horses. Then they set up a lot of banners and flags, and kept the fires burning constantly, leading the horses out by night to join up with the other camp of Han dynasty loyalists.

Unaware of this, the Shu general led an attack south of the river the day after the two camps of Han loyalists had secretly joined together. The loyalists fought back with their whole force. The fighting continued from morning until evening, but the loyalists finally routed the Shu army and killed its two generals.

Now the imperial Han general led his troops back to his base of operations and left the other camp of loyalists there to oppose the self-proclaimed king of Shu himself. The general reported everything to the emperor, severely blaming himself for not having followed the emperor's directions from the start.

The emperor replied, "You were quite right to return to your base of operations in Shu. The king of Shu will surely not

dare to attack both you and the other loyalist army. If he attacks
the others first, you send your whole infantry and cavalry at him
from your base within Shu. When he finds he is in danger and
at an impasse, you will surely beat him."

Now the Han loyalist general did battle with the king of
Shu on the ground between the Han outpost and the capital of
Shu. They fought eight times, with the imperial Han loyalists
winning all eight battles, finally driving the Shu army back
behind the walls of the capital city.

At this point, the king of Shu himself led ten thousand
men out of the city for an all-out battle. The Han general sent
two huge contingents of elite troops to attack the Shu forces.
The army of the king of Shu took a thrashing and ran away. One
of the Han commanders, charging right into the fray, stabbed
the king of Shu to death.

The next day the city capitulated. The head of the self-
proclaimed king of Shu was chopped off and sent to the imperial
capital of China. Thus ended the civil war in the region of Shu
in the early days of the renewed Han dynasty, the so-called
eastern or latter Han, which lasted for another two hundred
years.

Hunger and Battle

Liu Ji said:

Whenever you mobilize an army on a punitive expedition
and penetrate deep into enemy territory, if you lack for provisions you will need to send troops out to plunder. If you take
over enemy storehouses and stockpiles, using their supplies to
feed your army, then you will win.

The rule is "By feeding off the enemy, you can be sufficient
in both arms and provisions" (Sun Tzu, *The Art of War,* "Doing
Battle").

During the period of the Northern and Southern dynasties, a
general of the northern Zhou dynasty led an army across the
river to take the territory of the Chen dynasty in the south. One
of the generals of the Chen dynasty led an army to strike the
Zhou invaders.

It was autumn, and the rains caused the river to flood,

cutting off supply routes. The men of Zhou were worried, but their general sent out troops to plunder what they needed for the army.

Now the Zhou general was afraid that the Chen general would realize he was short of supplies, so he had a large mound of earth raised in his camp and had the mound covered with grain, to make it look like a huge pile of grain. He then invited people from the local villages on the pretext of asking after their welfare; he let the villagers see the artificial grain pile and then sent them away.

As a result, the Chen general heard about the great heap of grain and thought it was real. The Zhou general also built more fortifications and set up barracks, showing that he was ready for a protracted campaign.

Now agriculture was ruined in that area, and the Chen general was at a loss. At first local people rode fast boats with supplies of grain for the Chen army, but the Zhou general devised a scheme to put a stop to this. He sent boats to the Chen army, boats that had been disguised to look like the supply boats of the local people, but which in reality concealed ambushers.

The Chen soldiers, seeing the boats coming down the river and thinking they carried food, plunged into the current in their eagerness. Instead the ambushers hidden in the boats captured them.

There were some dissidents in the Zhou army who defected to the Chen side, and the Chen general took them all in. The general of Zhou took a horse to a boat, then had someone in the boat whip it; he repeated this several times, until the horse learned to fear boats and would not board. Then he stationed some ambushers along the river bank, and sent a pretended defector to the Chen general, mounted on the horse that feared boats.

When the Chen general sent some men to greet the defector, they vied with each other to get the horse. But the horse took fright and wouldn't board the boat with the soldiers; and in the commotion the Zhou ambushers rose from their hiding places along the river bank and killed every one of the men sent by the Chen general.

Later, when real supply boats or real defectors came along, the Chen general feared it was another Zhou ambush and wouldn't take them in. Thus there was a standoff for more than a year, and the Chen army was ultimately unable to stop the Zhou invaders.

Fighting on Full Stomachs

Liu Ji said:

When enemies come from far away and their supplies do not last, then they are hungry while you are well fed. In such a situation you should strengthen your defenses and not engage in battle. Hold them at a standoff so long that they wear out. Cut off their supply routes. If they retreat, send bushwhackers after them under cover to attack them by surprise on their way home; then you will not fail to beat them.

The rule is "Standing your ground awaiting those far away, awaiting the weary in comfort, awaiting the hungry on full stomachs, is mastering strength" (Sun Tzu, *The Art of War*, "Armed Struggle").

The Tang dynasty, during which China was a leader of world civilizations in the arts and sciences, lasted nearly three hundred years. It was formally established in the year 618, supplanting the Sui dynasty.

The Sui dynasty is distinguished for having unified China after the protracted civil wars of the era of the Northern and Southern dynasties. The heir of the founder of Sui, however, used his inherited power to undertake aggressive imperialist campaigns that alienated the people and brought the dynasty to a swift destruction. After the Sui collapsed, the warlord-administrators of the new empire, which had never been fully demilitarized, were foremost among those who scrambled for the power relinquished by the house of the Sui.

One of the Sui warlords continued to occupy a certain area even after the founding of the Tang dynasty had been formally proclaimed elsewhere. With the help of Central Asian Turks, the Sui warlord inflicted a series of defeats on the Tang armies. The warlord was so successful that he even sent one of his generals into Tang territory to expand his own bailiwick.

As a result, the founder of the Tang dynasty led an expedition against the Sui warlord in the year 619. The Tang warrior-prince, who established the dynasty and set his father on the throne, told his own generals, "The Sui warlord's general is deep in our territory, along with all their elite troops and best commanders. It seems to me, however, that while their army is large, they must really be short of supplies, seeing as how they are plundering to sustain themselves. Their intention is to do battle quickly. We should strengthen our fortifications and wait for them to starve. We shouldn't rush into a fight."

The Tang forces followed the reasoning of their leader, strengthening their defenses while cutting off enemy supply lines. Eventually they starved out the Sui army.

Fatigue and Battle

Liu Ji said:

In warfare, if there is an advantageous position but the enemy has already occupied it, if you then head into battle there you will be fatigued and therefore suffer defeat at the hands of the enemy.

The rule is "Those who are first on the battlefield and await opponents are at ease; those who are last on the battlefield and head into battle get worn out" (Sun Tzu, *The Art of War*, "Emptiness and Fullness").

After the civil wars of the Three Kingdoms period, the Jin dynasty was established, supplanting the victorious kingdom of Wei. The Jin dynasty lasted from 265 to 420, but it was challenged by a series of kingdoms ruled by non-Chinese peoples. These latter were called the Sixteen Kingdoms, and they were established by warlord-kings from among five Central Asian minorities who adopted elements of the cultures of East and South Asia in their rise to nationhood.

In the early fourth century, a high minister of the Jin dynasty sent an army of more than one hundred thousand troops to attack one of these kingdoms, which was ruled by a race of people known in Chinese as Jie, descendants of the ancient Xiongnu Huns.

The leader of the Jie intended to resist aggressively, but

someone warned him, "The Chinese army is well trained and powerful; it is impossible to stand up to it. For now let us strengthen our defensive positions and thus 'break their edge.' There is a difference in the power of attack and the power of defense; if we remain on the defensive for now we will gain complete victory."

But the Jie leader said, "The Chinese army has come from afar; the soldiers are physically exhausted and in a ragged and disorderly condition. We can beat them in one battle—how strong can they be? How can we let them go, when we have the opportunity to attack them before reinforcements arrive? If we draw back now and the Chinese take advantage of our withdrawal to attack us once our army is in motion, it will be every man for himself—then how can we fortify our defensive position? What you are recommending is a way to self-destruction without even a fight."

And in the end the leader of the Jie killed the man who objected to aggressive defense against the Chinese.

Now the Jie warrior-king appointed a vanguard commander and ordered that any laggards be executed. He set up a dummy force on top of a hill, then stationed two ambush forces on either side. The warrior-king personally led a brigade to meet the Chinese in battle, and then pretended to flee.

The Chinese commander sent his men to chase the Jie warriors as they fled. Now hidden Jie ambushers rose up and attacked the pursuers. The Chinese were routed and had to retreat.

Victory in Battle

Liu Ji said:

When you defeat enemies in battle, it will not do to become haughty and rest on your laurels; you should be strictly prepared for adversaries at all times. Then even if enemies do attack, you will be ready and will not suffer harm.

The rule is "Once you have prevailed, be as if you had not" ("Sima's Art of War").

The brief but momentous Qin dynasty (246–207 B.C.E.) put an end to centuries of civil war and unified China for the first time in more than five hundred years. The founder of Qin supplanted the self-cannibalizing feudalism of ancient China with civil bureaucracy and rule of law, unifying both material and intellectual culture in China to an unprecedented degree. The Qin also expanded its influence beyond the realm of ancient China and established the first Chinese empire.

The second emperor, who did not have all of his father's qualities, exhausted the new empire very rapidly with his imperial schemes. Thus there was intense discontent in many parts of China, and the Qin dynasty was overthrown in its second generation by widespread rebellions.

One of the leaders of a major peasant uprising sent two of his most powerful allies against strategic Qin positions, and they scored a series of victories over the imperial armies. As a result, the rebel leader began to take the Qin armies lightly, and he became somewhat haughty.

Someone advised the rebel leader, "Having prevailed in battle, if the commanders become haughty and the soldiers become lax, they will inevitably suffer defeat. Now your soldiers are getting a bit lazy, while the Qin forces grow by the day. I fear them for your sake."

The rebel leader, however, would not listen. He sent this advisor as an emissary to another state. On the way, this emissary met an ambassador from that very state, and asked him if he were going to see the rebel leader.

When the ambassador replied in the affirmative, the emissary of the rebel leader said, "Our leader's army is now headed for certain defeat; if you go slowly you will escape death, but if you go quickly you will meet disaster."

As it turned out, the imperial Qin forces launched a total assault on the peasant army, inflicting a crushing defeat on the rebels. The leader of the uprising lost his life.

Defeat in Battle

Liu Ji said:

When you are defeated by enemies in battle, do not fear. You should think of how to find benefit in having suffered harm: service your equipment, rouse your soldiers, and watch for the enemy to slack off so that you can attack. Then you will prevail.

The rule is "Through injury trouble can be resolved" (Sun Tzu, *The Art of War*, "Adaptations," Liu Ji's own paraphrase).

In the early fourth century, there took place the infamous "Riots of the Eight Kings," civil wars among feudal kings of the Chinese empire under the Jin dynasty.

At one point, the king of Hojian sent one of his generals to attack the king of Changsha. The emperor of the Jin dynasty personally sent a force to oppose the Hojian army, but a division of Hojian guerrilla fighters broke through the imperial army. Then the Hojian army entered the ancient capital of China.

Now the emperor's general, following orders, went after the Hojian army in the capital city. When the Hojian soldiers saw the imperial cavalcade in the distance, they began to have fears, and their commander could not stop them. Ultimately the demoralized Hojian forces suffered a crushing defeat, with the dead and wounded filling the streets.

The Hojian general retreated to an outlying position. Everyone was broken in spirit and had no more will to fight. Many of them urged the Hojian general to flee by night.

The general, however, responded, "It is a matter of course for there to be victory and defeat in a military action. What is important is to use failure to achieve success. We will press further forward and construct fortifications, then attack them when they least expect it. This is how to use surprise tactics in a military operation."

So that very night the remaining Hojian forces advanced under cover to a position very near to the capital city. The leader of the imperial army, meanwhile, having just won a resounding victory, didn't pay much attention to these maneuvers. But then when he suddenly heard that siege fortifications had been built outside the city, he led his troops out to fight. In the end, the imperial army was soundly beaten and had to retreat.

Taking the Initiative

Liu Ji said:

In war, when you perceive a reasonable possibility of

conquering the enemy, then it is appropriate to strike quickly. Then you can win every time.

The rule is "Proceed when you see it to be appropriate" (Wu Qi, "Assessing the Enemy").

In the early days of the Tang dynasty, one of the leading Tang generals dealt a telling blow to the Turks. The Turkish khan fled to safety in the mountains, then sent an ambassador to the Tang court to apologize and request that the Chinese empire accept the fealty of the Turks.

The Tang court sent the same general to welcome the Turks. But while the khan outwardly sought to have his allegiance accepted, he still had doubts in his mind, and the Chinese general sensed this. Meanwhile, the Tang court also sent an ambassador to the Turks to reassure them.

Now the Chinese general said to one of his chief assistant commanders, "When our ambassador arrives, the Turks will surely feel secure. If we send out a cavalry to attack them now, we will surely gain our desire."

The assistant commander said, "But the emperor has already accepted the Turks' surrender, and our own ambassador will be among them—what about that?"

The general said, "This is an opportunity not to be lost— why hold back just to spare the ambassador's life?"

Then the Chinese general quickly mobilized his troops and set out to ride on the Turks. They encountered over a thousand Turkish scouts on the way and took them all captive.

When the Turkish khan saw the ambassador of the imperial Tang court, he was very happy and did not worry about the Chinese army. The Chinese vanguard, meanwhile, took advantage of fog to advance, and the khan was not aware of their imminent attack until they were just a few miles away.

The Turks had not even had enough time to array their battle lines when the Chinese army struck them. The Chinese beheaded over ten thousand Turks and took more than a hundred thousand men and women captive, including the son of the khan himself.

The Chinese also caught and killed one of the princesses of the Sui dynasty, which had preceded the Tang as the ruling house of China. This princess had been actively encouraging the Turks to attack the Tang Chinese, hoping thereby to reestablish the Sui dynasty.

The Turkish khan fled, but he was subsequently captured and presented to the Tang court. Now Chinese territory was expanded all the way to the great desert.

Provocation and Battle

Liu Ji said:

In warfare, when your encampments and those of your enemies are far apart and your forces are of equal strength, you may send out light cavalry to provoke them, waiting in ambush for them to respond. By these tactics, their armies can be beaten. If enemies try the same strategy on you, don't attack them with your whole army.

The rule is "When the enemy is far away but tries to provoke hostilities, he wants you to move forward" (Sun Tzu, *The Art of War*, "Maneuvering Armies").

Concurrent with the Chinese Jin dynasty (third to fifth centuries) were sixteen kingdoms ruled by five different Central Asian peoples. These kingdoms included former Chinese territory within their domains and adopted certain elements of Chinese culture. This story concerns a conflict between two of these kingdoms, one under the leadership of the Qiang, ancient relatives of the modern Tibetans, and the Di, another ancient people who became increasingly Sinicized during the Jin dynasty.

The Di ruler sent two of his generals with infantry and cavalry to attack the Qiang, who were occupying a walled city in northern China. The Qiang, however, responded to this provocation by simply strengthening the city's fortifications, refusing to come out and fight.

One of the Qiang generals said, "The Di commander is a stubborn and inflexible man, easy to annoy. If we send a long line of troops to apply direct pressure to his defensive position, he will surely get angry and come out to oppose us. We can take him in one battle."

The other generals agreed, so they sent three thousand

Qiang horsemen and soldiers to the very threshold of the Di encampment. The leader of the Di was infuriated and sent all of his best troops out to fight.

The Qiang brigade pretended to be overwhelmed and withdrew, with the Di in hot pursuit. Just as the Di overtook the Qiang, the Qiang turned around and lashed back. Now the main Qiang force also arrived, and there was a tremendous battle. The Qiang killed the Di commander and took all of his troops prisoner.

Slow-Paced Battle

Liu Ji said:

The general rule for besieging walled cities is that it is to be considered the tactic of last resort, to be done only when there is no other choice. Even if the city walls are high and the moats are deep, if there are many men defending it but few supplies and no reinforcements from outside, then it can be taken by stranglehold.

The rule is "Move slowly as a forest" (Sun Tzu, *The Art of War*, "Armed Struggle").

During the era of the Sixteen Kingdoms, the Early Yan dynasty was established by a leader of the Xianbei people in the year 337. At one point in this turbulent period, the king of Yan found it necessary to fight the self-proclaimed king of Qi, a warlord who had inherited his father's army and pledged fealty to Jin-dynasty China to the east. After proclaiming himself king of Qi, as a vassal of China the warlord-king made war on the Xianbei kingdom of Early Yan.

The Yan forces surrounded the king of Qi in a walled city in northern China. The Yan commanders wanted to attack the city as soon as possible, but their general said, "There are times when it is best to go slowly. If we are equal in power, but they have strong reinforcements outside, there is the possibility that we may get pinned between them, having trouble in front of us and behind us. In that case, if we were going to attack it would have to be done quickly.

"On the other hand, if we are stronger than they are, and they have no outside reinforcements, we should keep a stranglehold on them until they cave in. This is what *The Art of War* means when it says, 'Surround them if you have ten times their number, attack if you have five.'

"Now the army of the king of Qi is large, morale is still good, and they are occupying a secure citadel. If we all put forth every last bit of strength and attacked them with the greatest possible intensity, we could take the city in a month or two; but we would surely lose many of our soldiers.

"The essential thing is to be able to adapt."

So saying, the Yan general had a wall of bunkers built to keep watch over the city, until the Yan army finally strangled the stronghold and took it.

Swift Battle

Liu Ji said:

When you besiege a city, if the enemy has abundant supplies, few men, and outside reinforcements, it is imperative to attack quickly in order to win.

The rule is "In a military operation, extraordinary speed is valuable" *(Records of the Three Kingdoms)*.

During the era of the Three Kingdoms, when factions of the regions of Wei, Shu, and Wu competed for hegemony over the remains of the Chinese empire after the fall of the Han dynasty, at one point a general of Shu defected to Wei and was subsequently made military governor of an area called "New City." Before long, however, the new governor established relations with the kingdom of Wu and transferred his allegiance back to Shu, rebelling against Wei.

Now Sima Yi, a leading general of Wei, sent a secret military force to strike the traitor. His commanders said, "Now that he is connected with Shu, we should observe from a distance before making our move." But the Wei general replied, "He is unreliable and lacks a sense of duty. This is a time when loyalties are in doubt, and we should hasten to resolve matters before he has settled down."

So the Wei troops traveled by forced marches day and night to arrive at the outskirts of New City. Both Wu and Shu sent reinforcements to help the defector, so the Wei general divided his forces to resist them.

At the outset of these events, the defector had written to the chief strategist of Shu, "New City is so far away from the center of Wei that I will have my fortifications all ready by the time the emperor in Wei is informed of my actions. My commanders are well prepared, and my location is protected by natural barriers. The great general of Wei will surely not come himself, and even if his commanders come they cannot trouble me."

But then when the Wei force arrived, the defector informed the Shu strategist, expressing his surprise: "It has only been eight days since I made my move, and the Wei army is already at the city wall. How extraordinarily swift they are!"

There was an outlying citadel surrounded on three sides by water, and the defector had a wooden barricade built outside for extra protection. The Wei troops, however, crossed the water and smashed the barricade, pressing right up to the city walls.

On the tenth day, several of the defector's own men assassinated him and opened the gates of the city, surrendering to the kingdom of Wei.

Orderliness and Battle

Liu Ji said:

In warfare, if the enemy's ranks are orderly on the move and the soldiers are calm, it will not do to enter into battle with them too readily. It is better to wait for a change or stir within them to strike; then you can win.

The rule is "Avoiding confrontation with orderly ranks and not attacking great formations is mastering adaptation" (Sun Tzu, *The Art of War*, "Armed Struggle").

This story is related to the preceding story, about the general of the Three Kingdoms era who defected from Shu to Wei, became a military governor in outlying territory, then defected back to Shu but also had ties with Wu. At one point he even declared independence, with the diplomatic recognition of the king of Wu.

According to this story, the great Wei general Sima Yi

launched his expedition against the seceding defector when this took place. His forces came in secret across the river and surrounded the citadel of the traitor, but then they left that city and headed for the heartland of the region.

The Wei commanders said, "Surrounding the citadel without laying siege to it was not a good example to show the warriors."

The Wei general said, "The rebels are securely entrenched and want to take advantage of that to tire our army. If we besiege the city, we will be falling right into their trap. The rebels are massed here, so their homes are empty; if we head right for the local heartland, the people will be afraid. If they come to fight in fear, we are sure to beat them."

So the Wei army marched through in orderly ranks. When the secessionists saw the army, they came out after it and did actually try to face it. Then the Wei general had his own soldiers strike back at them, routing the rebels.

Energy and Battle

Liu Ji said:

Generals wage war through the armed forces, the armed forces fight by energy. Energy prevails when it is drummed up. If you can energize your troops, don't do it too frequently, otherwise their energy will easily wane. Don't do it at too great a distance either, otherwise their energy will be easily exhausted. You should drum up the energy of your soldiers when enemies are within a calculated critical distance, having your troops fight at close range. When enemies wane and you prevail, victory over them is assured.

The rule is "Fight when full of energy, flee when drained of energy" (Wei Liaozi, "Rigor of War").

During the Spring and Autumn era, the state of Qi attacked the state of Lu. The lord of Lu was about to go to battle when one of his warriors asked to accompany him. So the lord and the warrior rode to the battlefield in the same chariot.

Now the lord of Lu was about to give the signal for the war drums to stir up the soldiers, but the warrior said, "Not yet."

Then when the men of Qi had drummed three times, the warrior told the lord of Lu, "Now!"

The Qi army was defeated, and the lord of Lu asked the warrior how this had come about. The warrior replied, "Bravery in battle is a matter of energy. Once energy is drummed up, a second try makes it wane, and it disappears at the third. They were exhausted while we were full, so we overcame them."

This story was later told as a classic case of the weaker successfully opposing the stronger through mastery of energy.

Fighting on the Way Home

Liu Ji said:

When you clash with enemies, if they withdraw and head home for no apparent reason, it is imperative to observe them carefully. If they are in fact exhausted and out of supplies, you can send commandos after them; but if they are an expedition on the way home, you cannot stand in their way.

The rule is "Do not stop an army on its way home" (Sun Tzu, *The Art of War*, "Armed Struggle").

In the year 198, near the end of the Han dynasty, the warlord Cao Cao, who was to become one of the most powerful competitors for the remains of the Han empire, had one of his rivals surrounded when another rival sent reinforcements to oppose him. The reinforcements took up a position behind Cao Cao, guarding the passes through the mountains to cut off his way back.

Cao Cao's army couldn't go forward, and now it had enemies before and behind it. That night Cao Cao's men tunneled through the defiles to give the appearance that they were trying to get away. In reality they lay in ambush, waiting for the enemies to come in pursuit.

Cao Cao's rival came after him with his entire army, and Cao Cao's soldiers destroyed it in a surprise attack. Later Cao Cao told one of his advisors, "The enemy tried to 'stop an army on its way home,' and also fought with us on 'deadly ground,' so I knew we would win."

Pursuit and Battle

Liu Ji said:

Whenever you pursue people on the run, chasing beaten soldiers, you must make sure whether they are really fleeing or just feigning. If their signals are coordinated and their orders are uniformly carried out, even if they are running away in apparent confusion and chaos they are not defeated. They surely have plans for surprise attacks, so you must take this into consideration.

If, on the other hand, their signals are disorderly and uncoordinated, if all sorts of different orders and directives are hollered and shouted, then this is the real fearfulness that is felt in defeat. In such a case you may pursue them vigorously.

The rule is "When you pursue people on the run, do not desist; but if the enemy stops on the road, then think twice" ("Sima's Art of War," "Deploying Groups").

In the year 618, the founder of the newly declared Tang dynasty moved against one of the last warlords of the preceding Sui dynasty. One of the Sui warlord's generals, opposing the Tang founder, was severely beaten and put to flight.

The Tang founder chased down the Sui survivors and surrounded them. Many of the Sui commanders surrendered right then and there on the battlefield. The Tang founder gave them back their horses and let them go.

Moments later, each of the Sui commanders came riding back. Now the Tang founder knew the real condition of the Sui warlord. As the leader of the new dynasty advanced his troops to close in, he sent a diplomat to the warlord to explain the advantages of capitulation and the risks of resistance. The warlord finally surrendered.

The generals of the young Tang founder congratulated him, and took the opportunity to ask, "When you had the enemy on the run, you left your infantry and rode right up to the city ramparts without even taking any siege equipment. We were all in doubt as to whether we could take the city, yet you did— how?"

The Tang founder said, "The men under the command of

the Sui warlord's general are all outsiders, people from a completely different region. Although our army beat them, we didn't kill or capture too many. If we gave them time, they would all go into the city, where the warlord would take them in and treat them as his own—then they would not be easy to overcome. I knew that if we pressured them, the soldiers would all run away back to their homeland, leaving no one here to fight for the warlord.

"The warlord's spirit is broken with mortal terror; that is why he surrendered, out of fear."

Not Fighting

Liu Ji said:

When opponents in warfare outnumber you, or they are more powerful than you are, or when you are at a tactical disadvantage, or when they have come from far away but still have supplies, in any of these cases it will not do to fight with them. It is best to fortify your defenses and hold them off long enough to wear them down to the point of vulnerability.

The rule is "It is up to you not to fight" ("Dialogues of Li, Lord of Wei").

In the early years of the Tang dynasty, the founder of the new regime led an army against one of the warlords of the defunct Sui dynasty, a warlord who had joined forces with the Turks against the Tang armies.

One of the founder's cousins, a young man of seventeen who was later to be a minister of state, went with the Tang army. The two young men—the founder himself being only slightly older than his cousin—climbed the citadel of Gem Wall City, overlooking a deep valley, to observe the battle lines of the rebels.

The Tang founder looked at his cousin and said, "The rebels are coming to face me in battle counting on their numbers. What do you think?"

The younger warrior replied, "The thrust of this band of rebels is not to be met directly. They will be easy to foil by strategy, hard to contend with by strength. Let us secure our position so as to blunt their edge. They are a rag-tag mob and cannot last long. When their supplies start to run out, they will disperse by themselves. We can capture them without even fighting."

The Tang founder said, "Your perception accords with mine."

As it turned out, the Sui fighters fled by night when their food ran out. The Tang army chased them into the next country and put them to flight in one skirmish.

Avoiding Battle

Liu Ji said:

When you are at war with strong enemies, at first their energy is keen, while your momentum is weak, so it is hard to hold them off. Avoid them for the time being, and you can prevail.

The rule is "Avoid the keen energy, strike the slumping and receding" (Sun Tzu, *The Art of War*, "Armed Struggle").

In the year 189, one of the generals of the imperial armies of the Han dynasty was sent out to quell a group of dissidents who tried to secede from the empire. The secessionists had surrounded a walled city, and the general was appointed to put down their insurrection.

An imperial minister noted for his violent and cruel personality urged the general to proceed quickly, but the general said, "Even supposing victory in every battle, it is still better to win without fighting. Therefore Master Sun says in *The Art of War*, 'Skillful warriors first make themselves invincible, then watch for vulnerability in their opponents.'

"Now the city that the rebels have surrounded may be small, but it is well fortified and not easily taken. The secessionists have been making a powerful attack, yet the city has not fallen; so they must be tired. To strike them when they are fatigued is the way to complete victory."

The siege went on, but the city did not fall; completely worn out, at length the rebel army disbanded. Now the imperial forces went after them.

At this point, the imperial minister advised the general,

"As Master Sun says in *The Art of War,* 'Do not press a desperate enemy,' and 'do not stop an army on its way home.' "

The general refused to listen to the minister and went in pursuit of the rebels on his own initiative, delivering a crushing blow.

Surrounding Enemies

Liu Ji said:

Whenever you surround enemies, you should leave an opening to make it appear to them that there is a way to survive, thus causing them to relax their determination to fight. Thus can citadels be taken and armies be beaten.

The rule is "A surrounded army must be given a way out" (Sun Tzu, *The Art of War,* "Armed Struggle").

In the last days of the Han dynasty, the warlord Cao Cao surrounded a certain city. Enraged when the city refused to capitulate, Cao Cao swore, "When the city falls, we will bury everyone in it alive!"

The siege went on for days, but the defenders of the city still did not give up. Now Cao Cao's brother said to him, "A surrounded city must be shown a way out, a way to survival. Now that you have announced your intention to bury everyone alive, this has caused all the people to defend it for their own sakes. What is more, the city walls are strong and their supplies are abundant. As we besiege the city, our soldiers are being wounded; and time is dragging on as they hold out. Now we have stationed our troops outside a well-fortified city and are attacking enemies who will fight to the death—this is not good strategy."

So Cao Cao followed his brother's advice, and in this way he finally captured the city.

Surrender

Liu Ji said:

In war, if enemies come to surrender, it is imperative to see whether or not their intention is genuine. Observe them and keep on guard at all times. Give your commanders strict directions to keep the troops in a state of readiness. Then you will prevail.

The rule is "Accept a surrender as you would take on an opponent" ("Book of the Latter Han Dynasty").

In 197, the warlord Cao Cao attacked one of his rivals, who surrendered to him. After that, however, the conquered rival attacked Cao Cao out of spite, killing Cao Cao's nephew and eldest son. Cao Cao himself was struck by a stray arrow during the assault.

Now Cao Cao moved his troops. His rival came with a cavalry to raid Cao Cao's army, but Cao Cao beat him back. Finally this rival ran away to join another warlord.

Cao Cao said to his commanders, "When I overcame this rival of mine, my mistake was not to take hostages right away. See what has happened as a result and do not make the same mistake again."

Hardship

Liu Ji said:

Essential to generalship is to share the pleasures and pains of the troops. If you encounter danger, do not abandon the troops to save yourself, do not seek personal escape from difficulties confronting you. Rather, make every effort to protect the troops, sharing in their fate. If you do this, the soldiers will not forget you.

The rule is "When you see danger and difficulty, do not forget the troops" ("Sima's Art of War").

During the era of the Three Kingdoms, when the warlord Cao Cao of Wei returned from his expedition against the king of Wu, he left a garrison of about seven thousand troops under three of his commanders. Cao Cao himself now went on an expedition against the leader of a semireligious popular militia, leaving the garrison chief with sealed instructions. On the outside of the instructions was written, "Open this if the enemy comes."

Before long, the king of Wu brought his troops to surround the Wei garrison. So the instructions of Cao Cao were opened and found to say, "If the king of Wu comes, let two of our commanders go out to engage him in battle; let one commander stay in the citadel to defend it. The garrison chief is not to fight."

Most of the Wei troop leaders were in doubt about these instructions, but one of the top commanders said, "With Cao Cao away on an expedition, the enemy is certain to beat us. This is why Cao Cao left those instructions. If we strike back at the Wu troops before they close in on us, breaking the force of their momentum, then we can calm the minds of our troops. Once that is accomplished, we can hold the citadel. The potential for victory or defeat is in this one action—how can any of you doubt it?"

That night the Wei commander called for volunteers to go with him. Eight hundred soldiers came forward. He killed some cattle to provide them with a hearty feast, for the next day there would be a major battle.

At dawn, the Wei commander put on his armor and went out to fight. He plunged first into the enemy battle line, killing dozens of men and cutting down two of their leaders. Shouting his name, the Wei commander crashed into enemy lines, fighting his way to the king of Wu.

With the Wei commander cutting his way toward him through the warriors of Wu, the king was terrified. Not knowing what to do, he and his bodyguards ran to high ground, the king defending himself with a halberd. The warrior commander of Wei called to the king of Wu to come down, but the king did not dare to move. Then the king regrouped his soldiers and surrounded the Wei commander.

The Wei commander struck at the surrounding Wu soldiers left and right, then charged straight ahead and broke through, so that he and several dozen of his men were able to get out.

Now the rest of the surrounded Wei force shouted to their commander, "Are you going to abandon us?" The commander then broke back in through the surrounding Wu soldiers and got his men out. None of the Wu fighters could stand up to the warrior of Wei.

The battle went on from morning until midday, until the men of Wu lost their spirit. Then the Wei troops went back to the citadel to fortify their defenses. Now everyone calmed down and gladly obeyed the Wei command.

When the king of Wu besieged the citadel, he continued his attack for ten days without success. Finally he withdrew. The Wei commander gave chase and nearly captured the king of Wu himself.

Easy Battle

Liu Ji said:

The rule of offensive warfare is that those who go the easy way prevail over their opponents. If your enemies are garrisoned in several places, there will inevitably be some places stronger and better manned than others. In that case, you should keep your distance from their strong points and attack their weak points; avoid places where they have many troops and strike where they have few—then you will not fail to win.

The rule is "Good warriors prevail when it is easy to prevail" (Sun Tzu, *The Art of War*, "Formation").

In the latter part of the sixth century, northern China was under the rule of the Xianbei, a northern Asian people culturally and politically influenced by centuries of contact with Chinese civilization. Two kingdoms formed by Xianbei leaders, the Northern Zhou dynasty and the Northern Qi dynasty, fought with each other to expand their territories.

The Martial Emperor of Zhou attacked a certain province of Qi, but one of his ministers said, "That province is a critical strategic area, where elite troops are massed. Even if we besiege it with all of our might it may not be possible for us to get our way. Let us attack another area, where there are few warriors and gentle terrain, a place that will be easy to take over."

The Martial Emperor refused to listen to this advice, and ultimately failed to succeed in his undertaking.

Battle in Extremity

Liu Ji said:

In war, if you greatly outnumber your enemies, they will fear your military strength and flee without putting up a fight.

In such an event, do not chase them, for people will fight back in extremity. You should follow them slowly with an orderly army; then you will win.

The rule is "Do not press a desperate enemy" (Sun Tzu, *The Art of War*, "Armed Struggle").

In the first century B.C.E., during the Han dynasty, a Chinese imperial general moved against one of the tribes of the Qiang, an ancient relative of the modern Tibetan people. The Han general led his army up to the campgrounds of the Qiang, where they had been stationed for quite some time.

The tribal warriors, in fact, had been garrisoned there for so long that they had grown slack. Thus when they saw the huge Chinese army in the distance, they abandoned their equipment and ran away, intending to cross the river that formed a natural boundary to the area.

The road was narrow and cramped, and the Chinese general pursued the fleeing Qiang at a leisurely pace. Someone said to him, "We are going too slowly to follow up on our advantage." But the general replied, "This is a case where 'a desperate enemy is not to be pressed.' If we go easy, they will run without looking back; but if we rush them, they will turn around and fight to the death."

All of the officers of the imperial Chinese army agreed with the general.

When the Qiang tribesmen plunged into the river, hundreds of them drowned and the rest ran away.

Warring in Accord with Nature

Liu Ji said:

When you want to raise an army and mobilize it against criminals in order to give comfort to the people, it is imperative to do so according to natural timing. You will always win when you mobilize military forces against enemies under the following conditions: their leadership is benighted and their government policies are arbitrary; their armed forces are overbearing and their people are worn out; they drive out good and wise people; they judicially murder the innocent. Enemies like this can be beaten.

The rule is "You successfully carry out a punitive strike when you follow natural timing" (Sun Tzu, *The Art of War*, "Strategic Assessments," commentaries; also in "Sima's Art of War," "Determining Ranks").

The sixth-century Northern Qi dynasty was one of the short-lived reigns of the turbulent era of the Northern and Southern dynasties. It was founded by the younger brother of the assassinated king of Qi, a second-generation vassal of the Wei dynasty, which was a non-Chinese empire that included northern China in its territory. The Northern Qi dynasty lasted for only twenty-eight years, with six rulers of three generations.

The last emperor of Northern Qi was popularly called "The Sorrowless Emperor." He appointed dishonest and treacherous people to administer the rule of government and to sit on the board of his advisory council. All of these people had their own personal cliques, whose members thereby were given promotions that were out of order. Official posts were obtained by bribery, and people were oppressed and persecuted by arbitrary policies. There was also internecine conflict among the vassals, resulting in the judicial murder of innocent ministers.

The Martial Emperor of Northern Zhou (543–578) was also non-Chinese, a chieftain of the North Asian Xianbei people. Gradually seeing the signs that the Northern Qi dynasty was collapsing and going under, as soon as he saw its basis crumble like a landslide he took this opportunity to destroy it. The last emperor of Northern Qi capitulated to Northern Zhou, and his whole clan was exterminated.

Health and Warfare

Liu Ji said:

When you are at war, if your army has suffered a setback, it is imperative to examine the physical and mental health of the soldiers. If they are healthy, then inspire them to fight; if they are run down and low in spirits, then nurture their health for the time being, until they are again fit for service.

The rule is "Take care of your health and avoid stress, consolidate your energy and build up your strength" (Sun Tzu, *The Art of War*, "Nine Grounds").

The First Emperor of China, who united China in the third century B.C.E., was the founder of the imperial Qin dynasty. At one point in his conquests he planned to attack the ancient land of Chu and asked one of his commanders, a certain General Li, "I want to take Chu—how many troops will be needed?"

General Li replied, "No more than two hundred thousand."

Then the emperor put the same question to another commander, General Wang. General Wang said, "There have to be at least six hundred thousand."

The emperor said to General Wang, "You must be getting old! How can you be so timid?"And he appointed General Li to lead an army of two hundred thousand troops in an attack on Chu.

General Wang, not having gotten the job, announced that he was ailing and went into temporary retirement.

Now General Li attacked Chu and dealt the independent state a crushing blow. Then he withdrew his troops to take up a position to the west; but the men of Chu followed him, not pitching camp for three successive days, and finally routed the Qin army, killing seven captains and putting General Li to flight.

Hearing news of this, the emperor was wroth. He personally went to General Wang and insisted that he return to active duty. General Wang said, "I am a muddled old man; if you insist on employing me for this mission, I will need six hundred thousand men." This time the emperor agreed.

When the men of Chu heard of this, they mobilized all of their armed forces to resist the Qin army under General Wang. General Wang, however, just strengthened his fortifications and did not do battle. He gave his soldiers plenty of rest every day, allowing them to bathe and wash their clothing. He also fed them well and generally provided for their comfort, sharing in their lot.

After quite a while of this, General Wang asked if the soldiers were playing sports in camp. When he heard that they were, he declared, "Now they are fit for action!"

The men of Chu, unable to oppose the Qin army in battle, withdrew to the east. General Wang pursued them and struck them down, killing their leader and putting the soldiers of Chu to flight, achieving a settlement by military means.

(Continued on next page)

Shambhala: The Sacred Path of the Warrior, by Chögyam Trungpa.

The Shambhala Dictionary of Buddhism and Zen.

The Spiritual Teaching of Ramana Maharshi, by Ramana Maharshi. Foreword by C. G. Jung.

Tao Teh Ching, by Lao Tzu. Translated by John C. H. Wu.

The Tibetan Book of the Dead: The Great Liberation through Hearing in the Bardo. Translated with commentary by Francesca Fremantle & Chögyam Trungpa.

Vitality, Energy, Spirit: A Taoist Sourcebook. Translated & edited by Thomas Cleary.

Wen-tzu: Understanding the Mysteries, by Lao-tzu. Translated by Thomas Cleary.

Worldly Wisdom: Confucian Teachings of the Ming Dynasty. Translated & edited by J. C. Cleary.

Zen Dawn: Early Zen Texts from Tun Huang. Translated by J. C. Cleary.

Zen Essence: The Science of Freedom. Translated & edited by Thomas Cleary.

The Zen Teachings of Master Lin-chi. Translated by Burton Watson.

THE ART OF WAR
BY SUN TZU
TRANSLATED BY THOMAS CLEARY

"Thomas Cleary's translation of Sun Tzu's 2,000-year-old *The Art of War* makes immediately relevant one of the greatest Chinese classical texts. There's not a dated maxim or vague prescription in it. . . . Absorb this book, and you can throw out all those contemporary books about management leadership."—*Newsweek*

Widely read as a modern guide to the art of leadership, this Chinese classic of military philosophy was composed more than twenty-five hundred years ago. This new translation is distinguished by its clarity and its inclusion of well-chosen commentaries by five Chinese generals of ancient times. Cleary's translation helps readers to apply the principles of military victory to relationships in personal and business life and teaches how to bring about the desired outcome in all the challenges and conflicts of life.

Thomas Cleary holds a doctorate in East Asian Languages and Civilizations from Harvard University. He is the translator of many classical texts of Buddhism, Taoism, and *I Ching* studies.

The Art of War *is also available in an audio cassette from Shambhala Lion Editions*.